About This Book

Teaching problem solving just got easier! Your friends at The Mailbox® have compiled a resource of 40 high-interest activities that will help students make sense of mathematics and become more confident problem solvers. The tasks in *POW! Problem of the Week Grades 3–4* are designed to give students practice with a variety of problem-solving strategies and lots of different math skills. The activities—20 at each grade level—progress from easy to more challenging, making it easy for you to best meet your students' needs.

This book provides brief descriptions of ten different strategies, including sample problems and solutions.

In addition, there is a special two-page lesson on each strategy that you can use with the whole class to introduce or review that strategy. Each lesson consists of a teacher page and an accompanying student page that shows students step by step how to use the strategy.

Also included is a checklist of the problem-solving process that you can duplicate for students to keep in their folders, plus a handy generic rubric to help you with assessment.

Each of the 40 problem-solving activities consists of a colorful teacher page and a reproducible student page. The teacher page includes the following:

- the overall objective of the problem
- a list of problem-solving strategies students could use to solve the problem
- a list of math skills students will use to solve the problem
- a brief summary of the problem
- a list of important information found in the problem
- an answer key
- a bonus box answer key
- a list of helpful hints for you to share with students when they need help solving the problem

The student reproducible includes the problem and explains what the student should do to solve it.

Turn to this resource whenever you want your students to have a meaningful problem-solving experience that helps them make sense of mathematics!

Table of Contents

How to Use This Book

POW! Problem of the Week Grades 3–4 makes teaching the problem-solving process easy. It provides everything you need: helpful background information, engaging teaching lessons, exciting student activities, and a handy assessment rubric! Use this great resource in the following ways:

• **Have students practice the important steps of the problem-solving process (page 5).** Give each student a copy of "Solving the Problem" to keep in a folder. It lists the five key steps in the problem-solving process: read it, think it, solve it, write it, and review it. Have students use the guide with each problem in the book.

• **Assess students' understanding of the problem-solving process (page 6).** Make a copy of the rubric. Use it and students' written responses to help you assess their thinking during the problem-solving process and to check their understanding of each strategy.

• **Use the overview of the ten problem-solving strategies as a reference (pages 7–11).** Refer to this handy guide for a brief description of and sample problem for each problem-solving strategy.

• **Introduce or review key problem-solving strategies (pages 12–31).** Teach students how to use and apply the problem-solving strategies with ready-to-use lessons. For each lesson, make a transparency of the student reproducible, plus copy it for each student. Then just follow the directions on the colorful teacher page.

• **Make problem solving fun and exciting with high-interest problems (pages 32–111).** Select from activities that are arranged by grade level and progress in order from less to more challenging. Each activity consists of a page for the teacher and one for the student. Scan the teacher page to find the problem-solving strategies or math skills students need to practice. Read the problem summary and the important information found in the problem. Note that there are even hints to give students who get stuck while solving a problem! Remind students to refer to the steps listed on their "Solving the Problem" page. Use the problems in a variety of ways:

- • independent practice or homework
- • morning work or free-time activities
- • partner or small-group practice
- • weekly learning center activities
- • whole-group instruction
- • assessment

Solving the Problem

Complete each step below to help you solve the problem. On a separate sheet of notebook paper, write your responses to Steps 2–5.

1. Read It—Read the problem. Read the problem a second time to find information you didn't notice during the first reading.

2. Think It—Think about the problem. Then rewrite it in your own words. Next, list any information that may help you solve the problem.

3. Solve It—Use the information to help you solve the problem. Show your work on paper. Write the solution or answer to the problem in complete sentences.

4. Write It—Write a summary of how you solved the problem. Include the strategy or strategies you used. Also include any charts, diagrams, or drawings you may have created. Describe which strategies worked and which ones didn't. Also include whether you got help from another class-mate or a parent. Tell how that person helped you.

5. Review It—Does your answer make sense? Is it reasonable? If you think your answer is *not* correct, explain why. Then tell where you got stuck or made an error. Tell about the most important or most interesting thing you learned from solving this problem.

Write an Equation

Choose the Correct Operation

Solve a Simpler Problem

Logical Reasoning

Work Backward

Work Backward

Logical Reasoning

Solve a Simpler Problem

Choose the Correct Operation

Write an Equation

MATH RUBRIC

4
Identifies all of the important parts of the problem

Fully understands the math needed to solve the problem

Communicates mathematical thinking clearly and creatively in written work

3
Identifies most of the important parts of the problem

Understands most of the math needed to solve the problem

Communicates mathematical thinking clearly in written work

2
Identifies some of the important parts of the problem

Understands some of the math needed to solve the problem

Communicates some mathematical thinking in written work

1
Identifies few of the important parts of the problem

Understands little of the math needed to solve the problem

Communicates little mathematical thinking in written work

Problem-Solving Strategies

Act It Out

The act-it-out strategy involves having problem solvers either role-play or physically manipulate objects, such as paper squares, to help them develop a visual image of the problem's data. The strategy is especially helpful when students need to visualize spatial relationships.

Sample problem: Six paper squares—orange, red, yellow, green, blue, and purple—are arranged in 2 rows of 3 each. The orange square is to the right of the red square. The yellow square is between the green and blue squares. The red square is above the blue one. The green square is below the purple one. How are the squares arranged?

Solution:

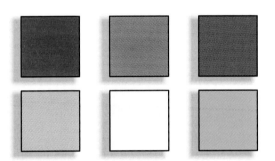

Draw a Picture or Diagram

Problem solvers use this strategy when a simple picture or diagram will help them visualize a problem. This strategy is especially helpful if a problem involves mapping.

Sample problem: Trevor left his campsite and hiked 6 miles south to the river. He then hiked 4 miles west to a cave. Then he turned north and hiked 3 miles to an old cabin. After he rests awhile, Trevor plans to hike east to pick up the first trail. When he leaves the cabin, how far does Trevor have to hike to reach the campsite?

Solution: The trail from the cabin to the first trail completes a rectangle, so it measures 4 miles. The distance from that point back to the campsite is 3 miles (6 miles – 3 miles). The distance from the cabin to the campsite is 7 miles (4 miles + 3 miles).

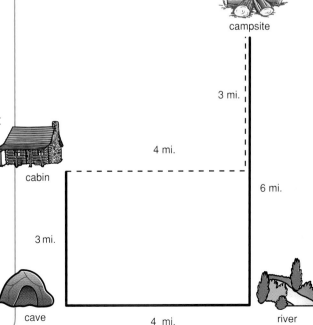

campsite

3 mi.

cabin

4 mi.

6 mi.

3 mi.

cave

4 mi.

river

Problem-Solving Strategies

Make a List, Table, or Chart

The strategy of making a list, table, or chart is often used when the information in a problem needs to be organized. Such organizers help problem solvers keep track of or spot missing data. Students can also discover relationships and patterns among the data.

Sample problem: Boards on Wheels is getting ready for its annual skateboarding contest. This year's contest has skateboarders from 3 different towns. For every 2 skateboarders from Oakdale, there are 3 skateboarders from Twin Oaks and 5 from Oakwood. If 40 skateboarders from Oakwood are in the contest, how many skateboarders from each of the other 2 towns will be there?

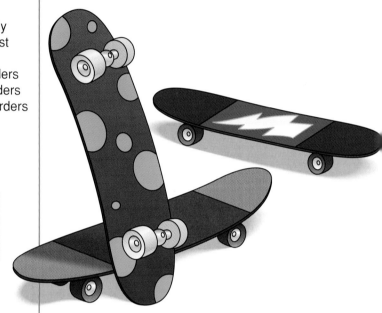

Solution: Oakdale—16, Twin Oaks—24

Oakdale	2	4	6	8	10	12	14	16
Twin Oaks	3	6	9	12	15	18	21	24
Oakwood	5	10	15	20	25	30	35	40

Guess and Check

The guess-and-check strategy is used when problem solvers need to make a reasonable guess about a solution. After a guess has been made, it is checked and, if necessary, revised. Each subsequent guess helps make the next one more accurate. In this manner, problem solvers gradually get closer to the solution by making guesses that are increasingly more reasonable.

Sample problem: All together, 25 children attended Marcus's Magical Show. There were 5 more girls than boys who came. How many boys and how many girls attended the show?

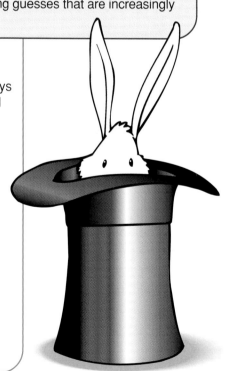

Solution: 15 girls and 10 boys
Problem solvers should guess a pair of numbers whose difference is 5 (for example, 12 and 7). Then they should check to see if the sum of those numbers is 25 (12 + 7 = 19). If the sum is too small, a second guess of larger numbers should be tried. If the sum is too large, a pair of smaller numbers should be tried.

Problem-Solving Strategies

Find a Pattern

The find-a-pattern strategy is helpful when problem solvers have to analyze a numerical, visual, or behavioral pattern in data and then make a prediction or generalization based on that analysis. It may require problem solvers to extend a pattern or make a table to reveal a pattern.

Sample problem: Detective I. M. Stumped depends on his dog, Sherlock, to help with his big cases. See if you can help this pair crack the code to the pattern below.

5 _____ = 13
20 _____ = 28
49 _____ = 57
17 _____ = __?__

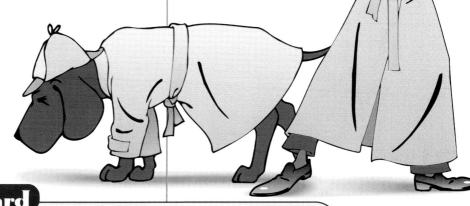

Solution:
5 **+ 8** = 13
20 **+ 8** = 28
49 **+ 8** = 57
17 **+ 8** = **25**

Work Backward

The work-backward strategy involves starting with the end result or data given at the end of a problem and then making a series of inverse computations to find the missing information.

Sample problem: It is 6:00 P.M., and Granny Smith is still shopping at the mall! She spent 45 minutes browsing through magazines in a bookstore, 40 minutes listening to CDs in a music store, and 1 hour dreaming about diamonds in a jewelry store. At what time did she begin shopping?

Solution: 3:35 P.M.
6:00 P.M. – 60 minutes = 5:00 P.M.
5:00 P.M. – 40 minutes = 4:20 P.M.
4:20 P.M. – 45 minutes = 3:35 P.M.

Problem-Solving Strategies

Logical Reasoning

The logical-reasoning strategy involves the use of conditional clues to help problem solvers arrive at a solution. Clues can be stated directly or implied. They can also be included in if-then statements. Displaying the data in a chart can help the problem solver work through the problem one statement at a time to arrive at the solution.

Sample problem: At the Carolina Cat Show, there's been a terrible mix-up. Every cat received the wrong ribbon! Read the clues below. Then match each kitty with its correct ribbon. Mark an X in a box to show each ribbon a cat should not receive.

Clues:

1. These cats received the wrong ribbons: Sam—Best Behaved, Gracie—Best Groomed, Tiger—Best Tricks, Precious—Fluffiest, Fluffy—Sweetest Meow.
2. Tiger was not well behaved.
3. Sam did the best tricks.
4. Neither Precious nor Fluffy won the ribbons that Gracie and Sam were given by mistake.

	Sam	Gracie	Tiger	Precious	Fluffy
Best Behaved					
Best Groomed					
Best Tricks					
Fluffiest					
Sweetest Meow					

Solution:

	Sam	Gracie	Tiger	Precious	Fluffy
Best Behaved	X	✓	X	X	X
Best Groomed	X	X	✓	X	X
Best Tricks	✓	X	X	X	X
Fluffiest	X	X	X	X	✓
Sweetest Meow	X	X	X	✓	X

Write an Equation

Problem solvers use the write-an-equation strategy when they need to write a mathematical sentence to model information in a problem.

Sample problem: Alex spent $5.00 playing video games and bought 2 candy bars to eat as a snack. The candy bars cost the same. If Alex spent a total of $9.00, how much did each candy bar cost?

Solution: $2.00

c = the cost of one candy bar
2 x c + $5.00 = $9.00
2 x c = $4.00
c = $2.00

Problem-Solving Strategies

Choose the Correct Operation

The choose-the-correct-operation strategy involves having problem solvers decide which mathematical operation to use: addition, subtraction, multiplication, or division. Identifying key words and phrases in a problem can suggest which operation is appropriate for solving a given problem.

Sample problem: Guests at a brunch ate 4 platters of cream-filled pastries. Each platter had 3 pastries. If the guests also ate 10 fruit-filled pastries, how many pastries did they eat in all?

Solution: (4 x 3) + 10 = 22 pastries

Solve a Simpler Problem

The solve-a-simpler-problem strategy is used when a problem is too complex for problem solvers to solve in one step. A problem can be simplified by dividing it into smaller problems to solve, by substituting smaller numbers for larger numbers, or by decreasing the number of given items. The simpler representation can then reveal a pattern or suggest what operation or process to use to solve the problem.

Sample problem: Big Al, better known as Alligator Al, sells plastic alligators at Gator Land Theme Park. He sold 235 of his plastic gators during the first week of July. Then he sold 183 toy gators during the second week and 212 during the third week. Big Al's goal is to sell 800 toy gators per month. How many toys does Big Al need to sell in the last week of July to meet his goal?

Solution: 170 toy gators
Problem solvers can use smaller numbers to help them decide what to do with the information in this problem. They should first add to find the total number of gators sold in the first three weeks and then subtract that total from the goal.

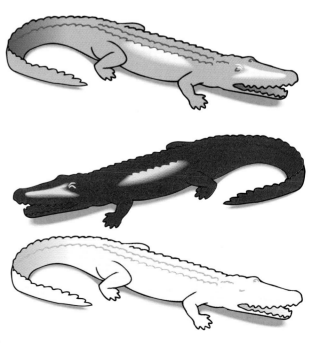

Lessons for Teaching Problem-Solving Strategies

Description of strategy: The act-it-out strategy involves having problem solvers either role-play or physically manipulate objects to help them develop a visual image of the problem's data. This strategy is especially helpful when students need to visualize spatial relationships.

Directions: Cut out the five jerseys at the bottom of the transparency. Label each jersey with a different runner's name. Then guide students to complete page 13 according to the instructions below.

Getting started: Have students read problem 1. Discuss the questions below one at a time, having students fill in the correct answers on their papers as you write them on the transparency.

- What are you to find out? *(the order in which the runners are lined up)*
- How many runners are there in all? *(5)*
- Where is Greg standing? *(in lane 1)* Gayle? *(directly to the left of Glenda)* Galen? *(between Glenda and Garth)*
- What does the word *directly* mean in the second sentence? *(Gayle and Glenda are standing side by side. There is no one between them.)*
- Is it hard to picture in your mind where all of the runners are standing? *(Yes, it's confusing trying to remember where each runner is standing in relation to the others.)*
- Would it help to use objects to stand for the runners and then move those objects around? Or would it help if 5 friends role-played the problem? Why? *(Yes, using real objects would make it easier to see the order of the runners. Having 5 people act out the problem would also be a good way to solve it.)*
- Which problem-solving strategy could you use? *(act it out)*

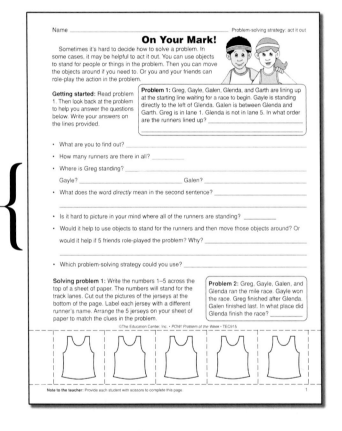

Solving problem 1: Have each student write the numbers 1–5 across the top of a sheet of paper. The numbers represent the five lanes of the track. Have each student cut out the jerseys at the bottom of the page and label each one with a different runner's name. Model how to look back at the clues and move the jerseys around to show how the runners are lined up. Then read the problem aloud, having students verify that the order shown below is correct.

Solving problem 2: Guide students through a similar procedure to solve the problem together as a class. Or have students solve the problem independently. Direct students to use the four cutouts labeled with the corresponding runners' names. Read the problem aloud, having students verify that the order shown below is correct. *(Glenda finished the race in 2nd place.)*

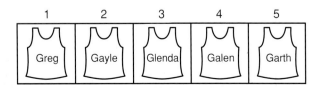

On Your Mark!

Sometimes it's hard to decide how to solve a problem. In some cases, it may be helpful to act it out. You can use objects to stand for people or things in the problem. Then you can move the objects around if you need to. Or you and your friends can role-play the action in the problem.

Getting started: Read problem 1. Then look back at the problem to help you answer the questions below. Write your answers on the lines provided.

Problem 1: Greg, Gayle, Galen, Glenda, and Garth are lining up at the starting line waiting for a race to begin. Gayle is standing directly to the left of Glenda. Galen is between Glenda and Garth. Greg is in lane 1. Glenda is not in lane 5. In what order are the runners lined up? _____ _____

- What are you to find out? _____

- How many runners are there in all? _____

- Where is Greg standing? _____

  Gayle? _____   Galen? _____

- What does the word *directly* mean in the second sentence? _____

  _____

- Is it hard to picture in your mind where all of the runners are standing? _____

- Would it help to use objects to stand for the runners and then move those objects around? Or would it help if 5 friends role-played the problem? Why? _____

  _____

- Which problem-solving strategy could you use? _____

Solving problem 1: Write the numbers 1–5 across the top of a sheet of paper. The numbers will stand for the track lanes. Cut out the pictures of the jerseys at the bottom of the page. Label each jersey with a different runner's name. Arrange the 5 jerseys on your sheet of paper to match the clues in the problem.

Problem 2: Greg, Gayle, Galen, and Glenda ran the mile race. Gayle won the race. Greg finished after Glenda. Galen finished last. In what place did Glenda finish the race? _____

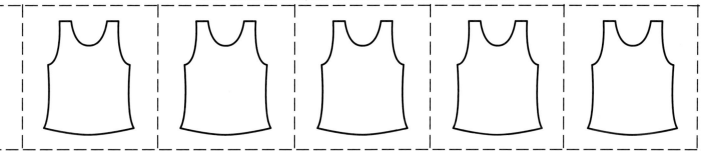

Lessons for Teaching Problem-Solving Strategies

Lesson 2: Draw a Picture or Diagram

Description of strategy: Problem solvers use this strategy when a simple picture or diagram helps them visualize a problem. This strategy is especially helpful if a problem involves mapping.

Directions: Guide students to complete page 15 according to the instructions below.

Getting started: Have students read problem 1. Discuss the questions below one at a time, having students fill in the correct answers on their papers as you write them on the transparency.

- What are you to find out? *(in which direction and how far the students will walk from the governor's home to their bus)*
- Where did the students begin their tour? *(at the capitol)*
- First, in which direction and how far did they walk to reach the history museum? *(north 6 blocks)*
- Next, in which direction and how far did the class walk from the museum to the park? *(west 4 blocks)*
- Finally, in which directions and how far did the students walk to get to the governor's home? *(south 14 blocks and then east 4 blocks)*
- Would it help to have a map that shows this information? *(Yes, a map would make it easier to see where all the sites are and figure out the distances between them.)*
- Which problem-solving strategy could you use? *(draw a picture or diagram)*

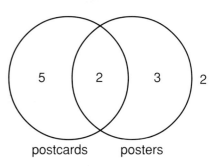

Solving problem 1:
Have students copy the part of the map that is shown. Then have them complete their maps by drawing and labeling additional line segments and the sites visited. Guide students to see that the completed map looks like a rectangle. Since one side of the rectangle is 14 blocks, the other side must equal 14 blocks. *(The fourth graders must walk north 8 blocks to return to their bus.)*

Solving problem 2: Guide students through a similar procedure to solve the problem together as a class. Or have students solve the problem independently. Remind students to label the diagram with the information that is available. *(Since there are 12 students in all and 10 are accounted for, the remaining 2 bought both postcards and posters.)*

Capital Capers

Drawing a picture or diagram is helpful in solving some types of math problems. Make and label drawings to help you solve each problem below.

Getting started: Read problem 1. Then look back at the problem to help you answer the questions below. Write your answers on the lines provided.

Problem 1: Mr. Fischer's fourth graders went on a field trip to their state's capital. When they arrived, the bus parked in front of the capitol where the tour began. From there, the class walked 6 blocks north to the history museum, then 4 blocks west to the park. The group continued its tour by walking 14 blocks south, then 4 blocks east to the governor's home. In which direction and how far will the students walk to get back to their bus?

- What are you to find out? _____

- Where did the students begin their tour? _____

- First, in which direction and how far did they walk to reach the history museum? _____

- Next, in which direction and how far did the class walk from the museum to the park? _____

_____

- Finally, in which directions and how far did the students walk to get to the governor's home?

_____

- Would it help to have a map that shows this information? _____

- Which problem-solving strategy could you use? _____

Solving problem 1: Draw a map on another sheet of paper to help you solve the problem. The map has been started for you. It shows where the students began their tour (the capitol) and the next place they visited (the history museum). It also shows the distance between these two sites (six blocks). Continue the map until you show the last place visited: the governor's home. Look at your map to see in which direction the capitol is from the governor's home. Then figure out how many blocks the students will walk to return to the bus.

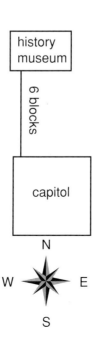

Problem 2: Twelve fourth graders visited the history museum's gift shop. Five of the students bought only postcards and 3 bought only posters. Some students bought both postcards and posters. Two students didn't buy anything. How many students bought both postcards and posters? Finish the Venn diagram below to help you answer the question.

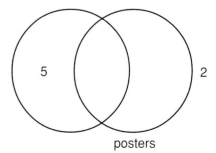

Lessons for Teaching Problem-Solving Strategies

Lesson 3: Make a List, Table, or Chart

(Description of strategy:) The strategy of making a list, table, or chart is often used when the information in a problem needs to be organized. These organizers help problem solvers keep track of or spot missing data. Relationships and patterns among the data may also be noted.

(Directions:) Guide students to complete page 17 according to the instructions below.

(Getting started:) Have students read problem 1. Discuss the questions below one at a time, having students fill in the correct answers on their papers as you write them on the transparency.

- What are you to find out? *(how many possible point totals Sir Miss-a-Lot could have scored)*
- How many arrows did Sir Miss-a-Lot shoot? *(3)*
- How many of those arrows hit the target? *(all 3 of them)*
- What is the point value of each target section? *(10, 7, and 3)*
- What is the most points Sir Miss-a-Lot could score? *(30)*
- What is the fewest points he could score? *(9)*
- How many points would Sir Miss-a-Lot score if one arrow landed in each section? *(20)*
- Are there other possible combinations of points that he could score? If so, how can you keep track of them? *(yes, by making a table and listing all the combinations)*
- Which problem-solving strategy could you use? *(make a list, table, or chart)*

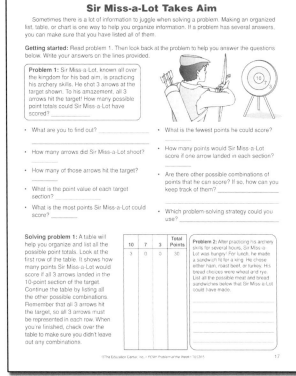

Solving problem 1: Have students continue filling in the table by showing all three arrows landing in the seven-point section and then with all three arrows landing in the three-point section. Ask students what would be the next best combination after three arrows landing in the ten-point section. *(2 arrows landing in the 10-point section and 1 arrow landing in the 7-point section).* After they have worked on the problem for a while, give the hint that there are ten possible combinations for Sir Miss-a-Lot's totals. Check students' answers by the table shown. The order may vary.

10	7	3	Total Points
3	0	0	30
0	3	0	21
0	0	3	9
2	1	0	27
2	0	1	23
1	2	0	24
0	2	1	17
1	0	2	16
0	1	2	13
1	1	1	20

Solving problem 2: Guide students through a similar procedure to solve the problem together as a class. Or have students solve the problem independently. Suggest that students list all the sandwiches that are possible with wheat bread and then repeat the process with rye bread. *(There are 6 combinations. See the list below.)*

wheat-ham	rye-ham
wheat-roast beef	rye-roast beef
wheat-turkey	rye-turkey

Sir Miss-a-Lot Takes Aim

Sometimes there is a lot of information to juggle when solving a problem. Making an organized list, table, or chart is one way to help you organize information. If a problem has several answers, you can make sure that you have listed all of them.

Getting started: Read problem 1. Then look back at the problem to help you answer the questions below. Write your answers on the lines provided.

Problem 1: Sir Miss-a-Lot, known all over the kingdom for his bad aim, is practicing his archery skills. He shot 3 arrows at the target shown. To his amazement, all 3 arrows hit the target! How many possible point totals could Sir Miss-a-Lot have scored? _____

- What are you to find out? _____

_____

- How many arrows did Sir Miss-a-Lot shoot? _____

- How many of those arrows hit the target? _____

- What is the point value of each target section? _____

- What is the most points Sir Miss-a-Lot could score? _____

- What is the fewest points he could score? _____

- How many points would Sir Miss-a-Lot score if one arrow landed in each section? _____

- Are there other possible combinations of points that he can score? If so, how can you keep track of them? _____

_____

- Which problem-solving strategy could you use? _____

Solving problem 1: A table will help you organize and list all the possible point totals. Look at the first row of the table. It shows how many points Sir Miss-a-Lot would score if all 3 arrows landed in the 10-point section of the target. Continue the table by listing all the other possible combinations. Remember that all 3 arrows hit the target, so all 3 arrows must be represented in each row. When you're finished, check over the table to make sure you didn't leave out any combinations.

10	7	3	Total Points
3	0	0	30

Problem 2: After practicing his archery skills for several hours, Sir Miss-a-Lot was hungry! For lunch, he made a sandwich fit for a king. He chose either ham, roast beef, or turkey. His bread choices were wheat and rye. List all the possible meat and bread sandwiches below that Sir Miss-a-Lot could have made.

_____

_____

_____

_____

Lessons for Teaching Problem-Solving Strategies

Lesson 4: Guess and Check

(Description of strategy:) The guess-and-check strategy is used when problem solvers need to make a reasonable guess about a solution. After a guess has been made, it is checked and then revised if necessary. Each subsequent guess helps make the next one more accurate. In this manner, problem solvers gradually get closer to the solution by making guesses that are increasingly more reasonable.

(Directions:) Guide students to complete page 19 according to the instructions below.

(Getting started:) Have students read problem 1. Discuss the questions below one at a time, having students fill in the correct answers on their papers as you write them on the transparency.

- What are you to find out? *(how many adults' tickets and how many children's tickets the Taylors bought)*
- How many tickets did the Taylors buy all together? *(5)*
- What was the total cost of the tickets? *($25.00)*
- How much is an adult's ticket? *($6.50)*
- How much is a child's ticket? *($4.00)*
- Would guessing help you solve this problem? *(yes)*
- If your guess is wrong, what can you do? *(try another guess and see if it works)*
- Which problem-solving strategy can you use? *(guess and check)*

Solving problem 1: First, have students add or multiply to find the most adult tickets that $25.00 will buy. If students guess four, they will see that four tickets cost $26.00. So that guess is too high. Next, suggest that students try three adult tickets. After computing, they will see that three adult tickets cost $19.50, leaving $5.50 for children's tickets. The cost of a child's ticket will not divide evenly into $5.50. Two adult tickets cost $13.00, leaving $12.00 for children's tickets. By dividing $12.00 by $4.00, students will see that three children's tickets can be purchased. *(2 adults' tickets and 3 children's tickets)*

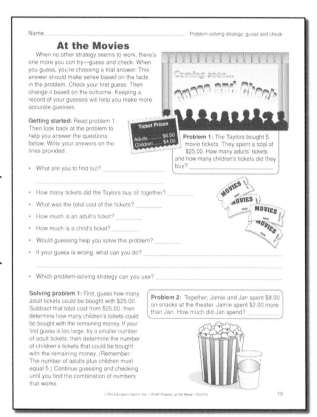

Solving problem 2: Guide students through a similar procedure to solve the problem together as a class. Or have students solve the problem independently. *(Jamie spent $5.00 and Jan spent $3.00—a total of $8.00 in all.)*

At the Movies

When no other strategy seems to work, there's one more you can try—guess and check. When you guess, you're choosing a trial answer. This answer should make sense based on the facts in the problem. Check your first guess. Then change it based on the outcome. Keeping a record of your guesses will help you make more accurate guesses.

Getting started: Read problem 1. Then look back at the problem to help you answer the questions below. Write your answers on the lines provided.

Ticket Prices

Adults $6.50
Children $4.00

Problem 1: The Taylors bought 5 movie tickets. They spent a total of $25.00. How many adults' tickets and how many children's tickets did they buy? _____

• What are you to find out? _____
_____

• How many tickets did the Taylors buy all together? _____

• What was the total cost of the tickets? _____

• How much is an adult's ticket? _____

• How much is a child's ticket? _____

• Would guessing help you solve this problem? _____

• If your guess is wrong, what can you do? _____
_____

• Which problem-solving strategy can you use? _____

Solving problem 1: First, guess how many adult tickets could be bought with $25.00. Subtract that total cost from $25.00; then determine how many children's tickets could be bought with the remaining money. If your first guess is too large, try a smaller number of adult tickets; then determine the number of children's tickets that could be bought with the remaining money. (Remember: The number of adults plus children must equal 5.) Continue guessing and checking until you find the combination of numbers that works.

Problem 2: Together, Jamie and Jan spent $8.00 on snacks at the theater. Jamie spent $2.00 more than Jan. How much did Jan spend? _____

Lessons for Teaching Problem-Solving Strategies

Lesson 5: Find a Pattern

Description of strategy: The find-a-pattern strategy is helpful when problem solvers have to analyze a numerical, visual, or behavioral pattern in data. They can then make a prediction based on what they discover. Problem solvers may need to extend a pattern or make a table to reveal a pattern.

Directions: Guide students to complete page 21 according to the instructions below.

Getting started: Have students read problem 1. Discuss the questions below one at a time, having students fill in the correct answers on their papers as you write them on the transparency.

- What are you to find out? *(how many pizzas Antonio will make on Thursday)*
- How many pizzas did Antonio make on Saturday? *(25)* Sunday? *(40)* Monday? *(55)* Tuesday? *(70)*
- How many more pizzas were made on Sunday than on Saturday? *(15)*
- How many more pizzas were made on Monday than on Sunday? *(15)*
- How many more pizzas were made on Tuesday than on Monday? *(15)*
- Do you see a pattern? Describe the pattern. *(Yes, the number of pizzas increases by 15 each day.)*
- How can you use this pattern to help you solve the problem? *(Continue the pattern for Wednesday and Thursday.)*
- Which problem-solving strategy could you use to solve this problem? *(find and continue a pattern)*

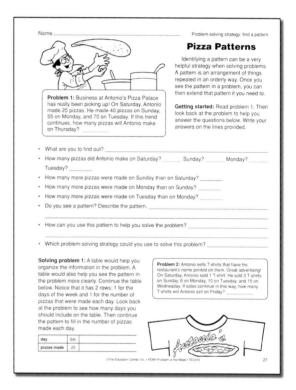

Solving problem 1: Ask students how many days should be listed in the table *(6)*. Have them continue the table through Thursday. Next, ask students to describe the pattern. *(Each day, the number of pizzas that Antonio makes increases by 15.)* Have students extend the table with numbers from the problem: 40, 55, and 70. Finally, ask students how they can determine the numbers that correspond with Wednesday and Thursday *(by adding 15 to 70 to get Wednesday's number—85 and then by adding 15 to 85 to get Thursday's number—100)*. Share the following table with students.

day	Sat.	Sun.	Mon.	Tues.	Wed.	Thurs.
pizzas made	25	40	55	70	85	100

Solving problem 2: Guide students through a similar procedure to solve the problem together as a class. Or have students solve the problem independently. Ask students to describe the pattern. *(On Saturday, 1 T-shirt is sold. Three T-shirts are sold on Sunday, 6 on Monday, 10 on Tuesday, and so on. The pattern is +2, +3, +4, +5, +6, +7.)* Share the following table with students. *(Antonio will sell 28 T-shirts on Friday.)*

day	Sat.	Sun.	Mon.	Tues.	Wed.	Thurs.	Fri.
T-shirts sold	1	3	6	10	15	21	28

Pizza Patterns

Identifying a pattern can be a very helpful strategy when solving problems. A pattern is an arrangement of things repeated in an orderly way. Once you see the pattern in a problem, you can then extend that pattern if you need to.

Getting started: Read problem 1. Then look back at the problem to help you answer the questions below. Write your answers on the lines provided.

Problem 1: Business at Antonio's Pizza Palace has really been picking up! On Saturday, Antonio made 25 pizzas. He made 40 pizzas on Sunday, 55 on Monday, and 70 on Tuesday. If this trend continues, how many pizzas will Antonio make on Thursday? _____

- What are you to find out? _____

- How many pizzas did Antonio make on Saturday? _____ Sunday? _____ Monday? _____ Tuesday? _____

- How many more pizzas were made on Sunday than on Saturday? _____

- How many more pizzas were made on Monday than on Sunday? _____

- How many more pizzas were made on Tuesday than on Monday? _____

- Do you see a pattern? Describe the pattern. _____
_____

- How can you use this pattern to help you solve the problem? _____
_____

- Which problem-solving strategy could you use to solve this problem? _____

Solving problem 1: A table would help you organize the information in the problem. A table would also help you see the pattern in the problem more clearly. Continue the table below. Notice that it has 2 rows: 1 for the days of the week and 1 for the number of pizzas that were made each day. Look back at the problem to see how many days you should include on the table. Then continue the pattern to fill in the number of pizzas made each day.

Problem 2: Antonio sells T-shirts that have his restaurant's name printed on them. Great advertising! On Saturday, Antonio sold 1 T-shirt. He sold 3 T-shirts on Sunday, 6 on Monday, 10 on Tuesday, and 15 on Wednesday. If sales continue in this way, how many T-shirts will Antonio sell on Friday? _____

day	Sat.	
pizzas made	25	

Lessons for Teaching Problem-Solving Strategies

Lesson 6: Work Backward

Description of strategy: The work-backward strategy involves starting with the answer given at the end of a problem. Then the problem solver must work in reverse to find the missing information.

Directions: Guide students to complete page 23 according to the instructions below.

Getting started: Have students read problem 1. Discuss the questions below one at a time, having students fill in the correct answers on their papers as you write them on the transparency.

- What are you to find out? *(how many baseball cards Hannah had in her collection to begin with)*
- How many baseball cards did Hannah sell? *(75)*
- What else do you need to know in order to solve the problem? *(how many baseball cards Hannah gave to her brothers)*
- How many brothers does Hannah have? *(3)*
- How many baseball cards did each brother receive? *(15)*
- All together, how many cards did her brothers receive? *(45)*
- How can you find the number of cards Hannah had to begin with? *(add 45 and 75)*
- Which strategy would help you solve this problem? *(work backward)*

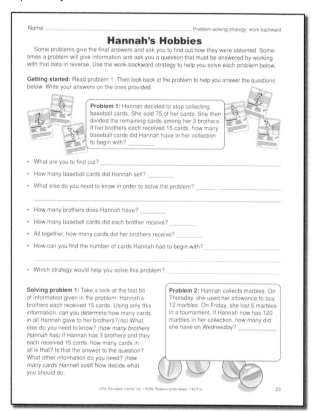

Name _____   Problem-solving strategy: work backward

Hannah's Hobbies

Some problems give the final answers and ask you to find out how they were obtained. Sometimes a problem will give information and ask you a question that must be answered by working with that data in reverse. Use the work-backward strategy to help you solve each problem below.

Getting started: Read problem 1. Then look back at the problem to help you answer the questions below. Write your answers on the lines provided.

Problem 1: Hannah decided to stop collecting baseball cards. She sold 75 of her cards. She then divided the remaining cards among her 3 brothers. If her brothers each received 15 cards, how many baseball cards did Hannah have in her collection to begin with? _____

- What are you to find out? _____
- How many baseball cards did Hannah sell? _____
- What else do you need to know in order to solve the problem? _____
- How many brothers does Hannah have? _____
- How many baseball cards did each brother receive? _____
- All together, how many cards did her brothers receive? _____
- How can you find the number of cards Hannah had to begin with? _____
- Which strategy would help you solve this problem? _____

Solving problem 1: Take a look at the last bit of information given in the problem: Hannah's brothers each received 15 cards. Using only this information, can you determine how many cards in all Hannah gave to her brothers? *(no)* What else do you need to know? *(how many brothers Hannah has)* If Hannah has 3 brothers and they each received 15 cards, how many cards in all is that? Is that the answer to the question? What other information do you need? *(how many cards Hannah sold)* Now decide what you should do.

Problem 2: Hannah collects marbles. On Thursday, she used her allowance to buy 12 marbles. On Friday, she lost 6 marbles in a tournament. If Hannah now has 120 marbles in her collection, how many did she have on Wednesday? _____

©The Education Center, Inc. • POW! Problem of the Week • TEC915   23

Solving problem 1: First, ask students how they can determine the number of baseball cards Hannah gave to her brothers. Then ask students what they should then do with that answer *(add that total to the number of cards that Hannah sold)*. The answer represents the number of baseball cards Hannah had before she began to get rid of them. *(Hannah had 120 baseball cards.)*

Solving problem 2: Guide students through a similar procedure to solve the problem together as a class. Or have students solve the problem independently. Guide students to understand that losing marbles means that those marbles are subtracted and that buying marbles means marbles are added. Ask students how many marbles Hannah had before she lost 6 *(126)*. Then ask how many marbles Hannah had before she bought 12 more *(114)*. Have students note that they perform opposite, or inverse, operations when working backward. *(Hannah had 114 marbles on Wednesday.)*

Name _____

Hannah's Hobbies

Some problems give the final answers and ask you to find out how they were obtained. Sometimes a problem will give information and ask you a question that must be answered by working with that data in reverse. Use the work-backward strategy to help you solve each problem below.

Getting started: Read problem 1. Then look back at the problem to help you answer the questions below. Write your answers on the lines provided.

> **Problem 1:** Hannah decided to stop collecting baseball cards. She sold 75 of her cards. She then divided the remaining cards among her 3 brothers. If her brothers each received 15 cards, how many baseball cards did Hannah have in her collection to begin with? _____

- What are you to find out? _____

- How many baseball cards did Hannah sell? _____

- What else do you need to know in order to solve the problem? _____

_____

- How many brothers does Hannah have? _____

- How many baseball cards did each brother receive? _____

- All together, how many cards did her brothers receive? _____

- How can you find the number of cards Hannah had to begin with? _____

_____

- Which strategy would help you solve this problem? _____

Solving problem 1: Take a look at the last bit of information given in the problem: Hannah's brothers each received 15 cards. Using only this information, can you determine how many cards in all Hannah gave to her brothers? *(no)* What else do you need to know? *(how many brothers Hannah has)* If Hannah has 3 brothers and they each received 15 cards, how many cards in all is that? Is that the answer to the question? What other information do you need? *(how many cards Hannah sold)* Now decide what you should do.

> **Problem 2:** Hannah collects marbles. On Thursday, she used her allowance to buy 12 marbles. On Friday, she lost 6 marbles in a tournament. If Hannah now has 120 marbles in her collection, how many did she have on Wednesday? _____

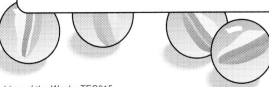

Lessons for Teaching Problem-Solving Strategies

Lesson 7: Logical Reasoning

Description of strategy: The logical-reasoning strategy involves the use of conditional clues to help problem solvers arrive at a solution. Clues may be stated directly or implied. They can also be included in if-then statements. Showing the data in a chart can help the problem solver work through the problem one statement at a time to reach a solution.

Directions: Guide students to complete page 25 according to the instructions below.

Getting started: Have students read problem 1. Discuss the questions below one at a time, having students fill in the correct answers on their papers as you write them on the transparency.

- What are you to find out? *(what school supply each friend bought)*
- How many friends bought supplies? *(5)*
- Which 2 friends can you match to their supplies? *(Trace and Meg)*
- Who did *not* buy crayons? *(Tim, Max)*
- Who did *not* buy paper? *(Cheri, Tim, Meg)*
- Would marking a logic box help you match the friends to the supplies they bought? *(yes)*
- Which strategy could you use to solve the problem? *(logical reasoning)*

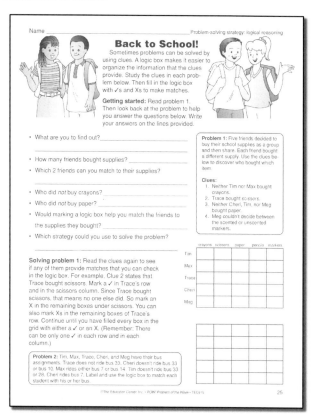

Solving problem 1: Guide students through the problem's clues.

- Clue 2 states that Trace bought scissors, and Clue 4 implies that Meg bought markers. So students should mark ✓s in the chart in the matching boxes. Remind students that when a ✓ is marked in a box, the remaining empty boxes in both that row and that column can be marked with Xs. (After solving Clues 2 and 4, students will have marked a total of 16 boxes in the grid.)
- When a clue states a negative ("*Neither* Tim *nor* Max bought crayons"), students should mark Xs. After marking Xs in Tim's and Max's boxes under "crayons," one empty box remains in that column: Cheri's box. So Cheri bought crayons.
- Since Cheri bought crayons, the remaining empty boxes in her row can be marked with Xs.
- Cheri bought crayons and Meg bought markers. Tim did not buy paper, so an X can be marked in Tim's box under "paper." Max bought paper and Tim bought pencils.

	crayons	scissors	paper	pencils	markers
Tim	X	X	X	✓	X
Max	X	X	✓	X	X
Trace	X	✓	X	X	X
Cheri	✓	X	X	X	X
Meg	X	X	X	X	✓

Solving problem 2:
Guide students through a similar procedure to solve the problem together as a class. Or have students solve the problem independently. First, have students label the chart with the five students' names and the five bus numbers. Check students' completed charts with the solution shown.

	7	10	14	28	33
Tim	X	✓	X	X	X
Max	X	X	✓	X	X
Trace	X	X	X	✓	X
Cheri	✓	X	X	X	X
Meg	X	X	X	X	✓

Back to School!

Sometimes problems can be solved by using clues. A logic box makes it easier to organize the information that the clues provide. Study the clues in each problem below. Then fill in the logic box with ✓s and Xs to make matches.

Getting started: Read problem 1. Then look back at the problem to help you answer the questions below. Write your answers on the lines provided.

- What are you to find out?_____

_____

- How many friends bought supplies? _____

- Which 2 friends can you match to their supplies?

_____

- Who did *not* buy crayons? _____

- Who did *not* buy paper? _____

- Would marking a logic box help you match the friends to

the supplies they bought? _____

- Which strategy could you use to solve the problem?

_____

Problem 1: Five friends decided to buy their school supplies as a group and then share. Each friend bought a different supply. Use the clues below to discover who bought which item.

Clues:
1. Neither Tim nor Max bought crayons.
2. Trace bought scissors.
3. Neither Cheri, Tim, nor Meg bought paper.
4. Meg couldn't decide between the scented or unscented markers.

Solving problem 1: Read the clues again to see if any of them provide matches that you can check in the logic box. For example, Clue 2 states that Trace bought scissors. Mark a ✓ in Trace's row and in the scissors column. Since Trace bought scissors, that means no one else did. So mark an X in the remaining boxes under scissors. You can also mark Xs in the remaining boxes of Trace's row. Continue until you have filled every box in the grid with either a ✓ or an X. (Remember: There can be only one ✓ in each row and in each column.)

Problem 2: Tim, Max, Trace, Cheri, and Meg have their bus assignments. Trace does not ride bus 33. Cheri doesn't ride bus 33 or bus 10. Max rides either bus 7 or bus 14. Tim doesn't ride bus 33 or 28. Cheri rides bus 7. Label and use the logic box to match each student with his or her bus.

	crayons	scissors	paper	pencils	markers
Tim					
Max					
Trace					
Cheri					
Meg					

Lessons for Teaching Problem-Solving Strategies

Lesson 8: Write an Equation

(**Description of strategy:**) Problem solvers use the write-an-equation strategy when they need to write a mathematical sentence to model information in a problem.

(**Directions:**) Guide students to complete page 27 according to the instructions below.

(**Getting started:**) Have students read problem 1. Discuss the questions below one at a time, having students fill in the correct answers on their papers as you write them on the transparency.

- What are you to do? *(write a multiplication sentence and then find the cost of 1 roll of film)*
- How much did Tamara spend at the camera store? *($12.00)*
- How many rolls of film did she buy? *(3)*
- Does the problem give the price of each roll of film? *(no)*
- Which strategy could you use to help you solve this problem? *(write an equation)*

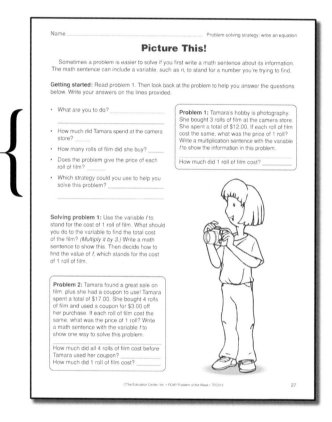

Solving problem 1: Guide students to write a multiplication sentence with the variable f to show the information in the problem: $3 \times f = \$12.00$. Then ask students the value of f. *($4.00)*

Solving problem 2: Guide students through a similar procedure to solve the problem together as a class. Or have students solve the problem independently. Have students note that the problem is similar to problem 1, except that Tamara is using a coupon. Ask students what happens when they make a purchase and use a coupon. *(The value of the coupon is subtracted from the cost.)* Guide students to see how the math sentence $4 \times f - \$3.00 = \$17.00$ shows the information in the problem. Next, ask students to figure out the total cost of Tamara's purchase before she used her coupon. *($20.00; if the total was $17.00 after subtracting the $3.00 coupon, then the total was $20.00 before using the coupon.)* Now that students know that the total was $20.00 and that four rolls of film were purchased, ask how much each roll of film cost. *($5.00; 4 \times \$5.00 = \$20.00)*

Picture This!

Sometimes a problem is easier to solve if you first write a math sentence about its information. The math sentence can include a variable, such as *n,* to stand for a number you're trying to find.

Getting started: Read problem 1. Then look back at the problem to help you answer the questions below. Write your answers on the lines provided.

- What are you to do? _____
  _____

- How much did Tamara spend at the camera store? _____

- How many rolls of film did she buy? _____

- Does the problem give the price of each roll of film? _____

- Which strategy could you use to help you solve this problem? _____
  _____

> **Problem 1:** Tamara's hobby is photography. She bought 3 rolls of film at the camera store. She spent a total of $12.00. If each roll of film cost the same, what was the price of 1 roll? Write a multiplication sentence with the variable *f* to show the information in this problem.
>
> _____
>
> How much did 1 roll of film cost? _____

Solving problem 1: Use the variable *f* to stand for the cost of 1 roll of film. What should you do to the variable to find the total cost of the film? *(Multiply it by 3.)* Write a math sentence to show this. Then decide how to find the value of *f,* which stands for the cost of 1 roll of film.

> **Problem 2:** Tamara found a great sale on film, plus she had a coupon to use! Tamara spent a total of $17.00. She bought 4 rolls of film and used a coupon for $3.00 off her purchase. If each roll of film cost the same, what was the price of 1 roll? Write a math sentence with the variable *f* to show one way to solve this problem.
>
> _____
>
> How much did all 4 rolls of film cost before Tamara used her coupon? _____
> How much did 1 roll of film cost? _____

Lessons for Teaching Problem-Solving Strategies

Lesson 9: Choose the Correct Operation

Description of strategy: The choose-the-correct-operation strategy involves having problem solvers decide which math operation to use: addition, subtraction, multiplication, or division. Identifying key words and phrases in a problem can suggest which operation is appropriate for solving a given problem.

Directions: Guide students to complete page 29 according to the instructions below.

Getting started: Have students read problem 1. Discuss the questions below one at a time, having students fill in the correct answers on their papers as you write them on the transparency.

- What are you to find out? *(how many cookies Leslie and Larry baked)*
- How many pans of cookies did Leslie and Larry bake? *(3)*
- How many rows of cookies did each pan have? *(4)*
- How many cookies were in each row? *(10)*
- How can you find out how many cookies were in each pan? *(multiply the number of rows by the number of cookies in each row)*
- How can you find out how many cookies there were in all? *(multiply the number of cookies in each pan by the number of pans)*
- Which strategy could you use? *(choose the correct operation)*

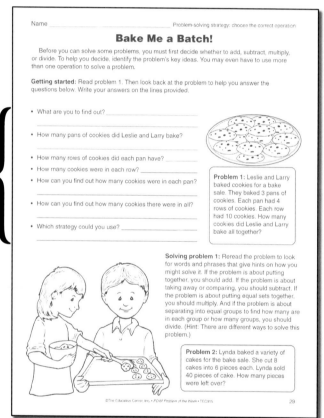

Name _____   Problem-solving strategy: choose the correct operation

Bake Me a Batch!

Before you can solve some problems, you must first decide whether to add, subtract, multiply, or divide. To help you decide, identify the problem's key ideas. You may even have to use more than one operation to solve a problem.

Getting started: Read problem 1. Then look back at the problem to help you answer the questions below. Write your answers on the lines provided.

- What are you to find out? _____
- How many pans of cookies did Leslie and Larry bake? _____
- How many rows of cookies did each pan have? _____
- How many cookies were in each row? _____
- How can you find out how many cookies were in each pan? _____
- How can you find out how many cookies there were in all? _____
- Which strategy could you use? _____

Problem 1: Leslie and Larry baked cookies for a bake sale. They baked 3 pans of cookies. Each pan had 4 rows of cookies. Each row had 10 cookies. How many cookies did Leslie and Larry bake all together?

Solving problem 1: Reread the problem to look for words and phrases that give hints on how you might solve it. If the problem is about putting together, you should add. If the problem is about taking away or comparing, you should subtract. If the problem is about putting equal sets together, you should multiply. And if the problem is about separating into equal groups to find how many are in each group or how many groups, you should divide. (Hint: There are different ways to solve this problem.)

Problem 2: Lynda baked a variety of cakes for the bake sale. She cut 8 cakes into 6 pieces each. Lynda sold 40 pieces of cake. How many pieces were left over?

©The Education Center, Inc. • POW! Problem of the Week • TEC915   29

Solving problem 1: Guide students to look for words and phrases that suggest key concepts. Point out that finding the number of cookies in each pan involves either multiplying *(4 x 10 = 40)* or adding *(10 + 10 + 10 + 10 = 40)*. Once the number of cookies per pan has been determined, guide students to see that they can either multiply *(3 x 40 = 120)* or add *(40 + 40 + 40 = 120)* to find the number of cookies that Leslie and Larry baked.

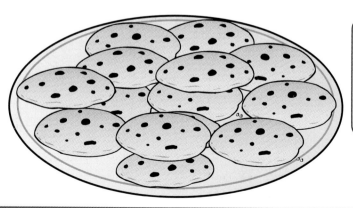

Solving problem 2: Guide students through a similar procedure to solve the problem together as a class. Or have students solve the problem independently. *(Lynda had 8 pieces of cake left over. Students should multiply 8 times 6 to get a total of 48 pieces of cake. Then they should subtract 40 from 48.)*

Bake Me a Batch!

Before you can solve some problems, you must first decide whether to add, subtract, multiply, or divide. To help you decide, identify the problem's key ideas. You may even have to use more than one operation to solve a problem.

Getting started: Read problem 1. Then look back at the problem to help you answer the questions below. Write your answers on the lines provided.

- What are you to find out? _____
  _____

- How many pans of cookies did Leslie and Larry bake?
  _____

- How many rows of cookies did each pan have? _____

- How many cookies were in each row? _____

- How can you find out how many cookies were in each pan?
  _____

- How can you find out how many cookies there were in all?
  _____

- Which strategy could you use? _____
  _____

Problem 1: Leslie and Larry baked cookies for a bake sale. They baked 3 pans of cookies. Each pan had 4 rows of cookies. Each row had 10 cookies. How many cookies did Leslie and Larry bake all together?

Solving problem 1: Reread the problem to look for words and phrases that give hints on how you might solve it. If the problem is about putting together, you should add. If the problem is about taking away or comparing, you should subtract. If the problem is about putting equal sets together, you should multiply. And if the problem is about separating into equal groups to find how many are in each group or how many groups, you should divide. (Hint: There are different ways to solve this problem.)

Problem 2: Lynda baked a variety of cakes for the bake sale. She cut 8 cakes into 6 pieces each. Lynda sold 40 pieces of cake. How many pieces were left over?

Lessons for Teaching Problem-Solving Strategies

Lesson 10: Solve a Simpler Problem

(Description of strategy:) The solve-a-simpler-problem strategy is used when a problem is too complex for problem solvers to solve in one step. A problem can be simplified by dividing it into smaller problems to solve, by substituting smaller numbers for larger numbers, or by decreasing the number of given items. The simpler representation can then reveal a pattern or suggest what operation or process to use to solve the problem.

(Directions:) Guide students to complete page 31 according to the instructions below.

(Getting started:) Have students read problem 1. Discuss the questions below one at a time, having students fill in the correct answer on their papers as you write them on the transparency.

- What are you to find out? *(how much more money Bryce needs to buy the bike)*
- How much money does Bryce have in savings? *($45.50)*
- How much more did he save in April? *($12.75)*
- How much money did Bryce earn in May? *($17.80)*
- How much was the check from Bryce's grandmother? *($15.00)*
- How much does the bike cost? *($95.00)*
- What is the first thing you need to find out? *(how much money Bryce has in all)*
- What clue in the problem tells you that Bryce doesn't have enough money to buy the bike? *(how much more money does he need)*
- Would replacing the numbers in the problem with simpler ones help you decide what to do? *(yes)*
- Which problem-solving strategy could you use? *(solve a simpler problem)*

Name _____   Problem-solving strategy: solve a simpler problem

Biking With Bryce

Some problems have information that is hard to understand. When you try to solve such a problem, think of a similar problem that is easier. Try to imagine a situation that is more familiar to you. Then think up easier numbers to use. This will help you decide which operation to use. Simpler numbers also make it easier for you to picture the action in a problem.

Getting started: Read problem 1. Then look back at the problem to help you answer the questions below. Write your answers on the lines provided.

Problem 1: Bryce wants to buy a new bike. He already has $45.50 in savings. In April he saved $12.75 more. In May Bryce earned $17.80, and in June his grandmother gave him a check for $15.00. If the bike that Bryce wants costs $95.00, how much more money does he need?

- What are you to find out? _____
- How much money does Bryce have in savings? _____
- How much more did he save in April? _____
- How much money did Bryce earn in May? _____
- How much was the check from Bryce's grandmother? _____
- How much does the bike cost? _____

- What is the first thing you need to find out? _____
- What clue in the problem tells you that Bryce doesn't have enough money to buy the bike?

  _____

- Would replacing the numbers in the problem with simpler ones help you decide what to do?

  _____

- Which problem-solving strategy could you use? _____

Solving problem 1: First, think of simpler numbers to replace the dollar amounts in the problem. For example: Suppose you have $5.00 and then you receive $1.00, then $2.00, and then $3.00. What would you do with those numbers to find out how much money you have in all? *(add)* What is the total amount? *($11.00)* Then suppose you want to buy something that costs $15.00. Do you have enough money? *(no)* How can you find out how much more money you need? *(by subtracting)* How much more do you need? *($4.00; $15.00 – $11.00 = $4.00)* So to solve problems like the one above, you can use smaller numbers to help you see the action more clearly. Then you can decide what to do with those numbers. To solve problem 1, first find out how much money Bryce has in all; then subtract that total from the cost of the bike.

Problem 2: Bryce's mom gave him the rest of the money he needed to buy his bike. Now he rides every day! He rode 43 miles the first week in July, 32 miles the second week, and 46 miles the third week. His goal is to ride 150 miles each month. How many miles does Bryce need to ride during the last week of July to meet his goal?

©The Education Center, Inc. • POW! Problem of the Week • TEC915   31

Solving problem 1: Have students note that there is a lot of information in problem 1: five pieces of data. Ask students to restate the problem in their own words without using any of the numbers. For example, they may say, "Bryce wants to buy a bike. He doesn't have enough money. How much more money does he need?" Next, ask students if they have ever faced a problem like this one in real life. Ask them what they must first do with the data provided. *(Add to find out how much money Bryce has.)* Continue by asking what they should do with that sum. *(Subtract it from $95.00—the cost of the bike.)* (Bryce needs $3.95 more in order to buy the bike.)

Solving problem 2: Guide students through a similar procedure to solve the problem together as a class. Or have students solve the problem independently. *(Bryce needs to ride 29 miles during the last week of July to meet his goal.)*

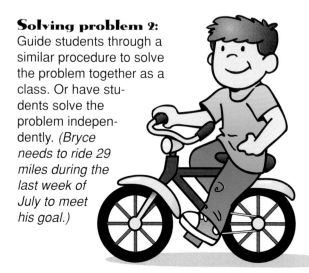

Biking With Bryce

Some problems have information that is hard to understand. When you try to solve such a problem, think of a similar problem that is easier. Try to imagine a situation that is more familiar to you. Then think up easier numbers to use. This will help you decide which operation to use. Simpler numbers also make it easier for you to picture the action in a problem.

Getting started: Read problem 1. Then look back at the problem to help you answer the questions below. Write your answers on the lines provided.

Problem 1: Bryce wants to buy a new bike. He already has $45.50 in savings. In April, he saved $12.75 more. In May Bryce earned $17.80, and in June his grandmother gave him a check for $15.00. If the bike that Bryce wants costs $95.00, how much more money does he need?

• What are you to find out? _____

_____

• How much money does Bryce have in savings? _____

• How much more did he save in April? _____

• How much money did Bryce earn in May? _____

• How much was the check from Bryce's grandmother? _____

• How much does the bike cost? _____

• What is the first thing you need to find out? _____

• What clue in the problem tells you that Bryce doesn't have enough money to buy the bike?

_____

• Would replacing the numbers in the problem with simpler ones help you decide what to do?

_____

• Which problem-solving strategy could you use? _____

Solving problem 1: First, think of simpler numbers to replace the dollar amounts in the problem. For example: Suppose you have $5.00 and then you receive $1.00, then $2.00, and then $3.00. What would you do with those numbers to find out how much money you have in all? *(add)* What is the total amount? *($11.00)* Then suppose you want to buy something that costs $15.00. Do you have enough money? *(no)* How can you find out how much more money you need? *(by subtracting)* How much more do you need? *($4.00; $15.00 − $11.00 = $4.00)* So to solve problems like the one above, you can use smaller numbers to help you see the action more clearly. Then you can decide what to do with those numbers. To solve problem 1, first find out how much money Bryce has in all; then subtract that total from the cost of the bike.

Problem 2: Bryce's mom gave him the rest of the money he needed to buy his bike. Now he rides every day! He rode 43 miles the first week in July, 32 miles the second week, and 46 miles the third week. His goal is to ride 150 miles each month. How many miles does Bryce need to ride during the last week of July to meet his goal?

Doubling Dimes

Identifying and continuing a money pattern

Problem-solving strategies

students could use:

- find a pattern
- write an equation

Math skills

students will use:

- double quantities
- add money

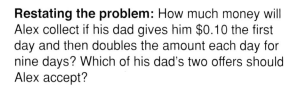

Restating the problem: How much money will Alex collect if his dad gives him $0.10 the first day and then doubles the amount each day for nine days? Which of his dad's two offers should Alex accept?

Important information found in the problem:

- The bike costs $89.96.
- The sale ends in ten days.
- Alex's dad has offered to give Alex half the cost of the bike.
- Alex's dad has offered to give Alex $0.10 today, $0.20 tomorrow, $0.40 the following day, and so on until the last day of the sale.
- Alex has $45.00 in his savings account.

(**Answer Key**) Alex will receive $102.30 ($0.10 + $0.20 + $0.40 + $0.80 + $1.60 + $3.20 + $6.40 + $12.80 + $25.60 + $51.20) if he chooses his dad's second offer.

Bonus Box answer: He will collect $57.32 more from the second offer than from the first ($89.96 ÷ 2 = $44.98; $102.30 − $ 44.98 = $57.32).

Helpful Hints

Share this information when students get stuck to help put them back on the path to correctly solving the problem.

Hint 1 Look at how much money Alex's dad will give him on the first, second, and third days. What pattern do you see? *(The amount doubles each day.)*

Hint 2 How many days will Alex's dad double the money? How do you know? *(9 days. The sale is over in 10 days.)*

Hint 3 Continue the pattern to figure out how much money Alex's dad will give him each day until the last day of the sale *($0.10, $0.20, $0.40, $0.80, $1.60, $3.20, $6.40, $12.80, $25.60, $51.20).*

Hint 4 How can you figure out how much money Alex will collect all together? *(Add the amount of money he collects for all 10 days.)*

Doubling Dimes

Alex had his heart set on buying a new bike. The bike was on sale for $89.96, but the sale was to end in ten days!

Alex asked his parents whether they would help him. His dad made two offers. First, he offered to give Alex half the cost of the bike. Second, he offered to give Alex $0.10 today, $0.20 tomorrow, $0.40 the following day, and so on until the last day of the sale. Alex could accept either offer.

Alex thought about the offers. He had $45.00 in his savings account. He could pay for half of the bike and then ask his dad to pay for the other half.

Or he could risk taking his dad's second offer. That way, Alex might not have to spend a dime!

Now It's Your Turn
Help Alex decide which deal he should take. Figure out how much money Alex will collect if his dad continues to double the money each day.

Bonus Box: How much more money will Alex receive from his dad if he takes the better offer?

Quimby's Quarters

Following a pattern to calculate money

Problem-solving strategies

students could use:
- find a pattern
- write an equation
- make a table

Math skills

students will use:
- add multiples of five
- add and multiply money

Restating the problem: Quimby will collect one of each state quarter the first year, two of each state quarter the second year, three of each state quarter the third year, and so on. How much money will he collect by the end of the ten-year period?

Important information found in the problem:
- Five new state quarters will be released each year.
- The first five state quarters were released in 1999. Quimby collected one of each quarter.
- Quimby decided to collect two of each state quarter the second year, three of each state quarter the third year, and so on.

Answer Key Quimby will collect $68.75 by the end of the program. (5 + 10 + 15 + 20 + 25 + 30 + 35 + 40 + 45 + 50 = 275 quarters, 275 x $0.25 = $68.75)

Year	1	2	3	4	5	6	7	8	9	10
Number of Quarters	5	10	15	20	25	30	35	40	45	50

Bonus Box answer: Quimby will have $35.00 at the end of the seventh year, 2005. ($35.00 x 4 quarters = 140 quarters, 5 + 10 + 15 + 20 + 25 + 30 + 35 = 140)

Helpful Hints

Share this information when students get stuck to help put them back on the path to correctly solving the problem.

Hint 1 How many state quarters are released each year? *(5)*

Hint 2 How many years will it take to release all 50 state quarters? *(10)*

Hint 3 Look at the pattern in which Quimby will collect quarters. How many quarters will he collect the first year? The second year? The third year? The fourth year? *(5, 10, 15, 20)*

Hint 4 Make a table to keep track of the number of quarters Quimby will collect. *(See answer key.)*

Hint 5 How many quarters will Quimby collect all together? *(275)*

Quimby's Quarters

Quimby Mint collects coins. He is especially wild about quarters.

Quimby was delighted when he heard about the 50 State Quarters Program. He found out that 5 new state quarters would be released each year.

Right away, Quimby began to plan how he would collect each of the new coins.

The first 5 quarters were released in 1999. Quimby collected 1 of each quarter. Then he decided to collect 2 of each quarter released the second year, 3 of each quarter released the third year, and so on.

Just the thought of all those quarters made Quimby feel like a millionaire! He grabbed a pencil and paper and started to calculate how much money he would have after collecting the quarters of all 50 states.

What a mountain of money it would be!

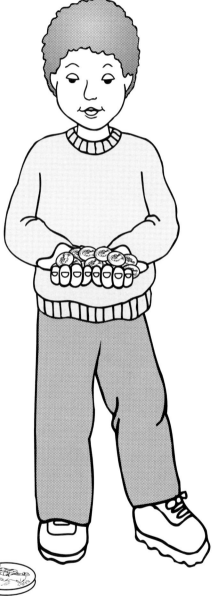

Now It's Your Turn
Figure out how much money Quimby will have by the end of the program.

Bonus Box: At the end of a particular year, Quimby will have collected a total of $35.00 in quarters. Which year will this be?

A "Tree-mendous" Rescue

Using a pattern to determine a tree's height

Teacher Page

Problem-solving strategies
students could use:
• draw a picture
• find a pattern
• logical reasoning

Math skills
students will use:
• count systematically

Restating the problem: Before the rescue squad can help Cottonball, it needs to know the height of the tree in branches. Use Cottonball's pattern of climbing up and down branches to help Catie figure out the tree's height.

Important information found in the problem:
• The ladders are built in the following branch heights: 20 branches, 25 branches, 30 branches, 35 branches, and 40 branches.
• The rescue squad asks Catie to figure out the exact height of the tree in branches.
• From the bottom of the tree, Cottonball climbed up seven branches and then down four branches. On her second move, she climbed up five branches and then down two branches. On her third move, she climbed up seven branches and then down four branches. On her fourth move, she climbed up five branches and then down two branches.
• Cottonball reached the top branch during her tenth move.

Answer Key The tree is 32 branches high. The rescue squad should bring the 35-branch ladder.

Bonus Box answer: Cottonball will be at the 51st branch after her 17th move. Cottonball climbs a net of 3 branches each move (17 x 3 = 51).

Helpful Hints
Share this information when students get stuck to help put them back on the path to correctly solving the problem.

Hint 1 On which branch was Cottonball after her first move? *(third branch)* Second move? *(sixth branch)* Third move? *(ninth branch)* Fourth move? *(12th branch)*

Hint 2 What relationship exists between the number of the move and the branch position? *(The branch position is 3 times the number of the move.)*

Hint 3 How can you predict the rule for Cottonball's movement based on the number of the move? *(If the move is an odd number, Cottonball will climb up 7 branches and then down 4 branches. If the move is an even number, she will climb up 5 branches and then down 2 branches.)*

Hint 4 On which branch was Cottonball after the ninth move? *(27th branch)*

Hint 5 How many branches did Cottonball climb up during her tenth move? *(5)* What was the highest branch Cottonball reached? *(32nd branch)*

A "Tree-mendous" Rescue

POW! #3

Catie's cat is in trouble! For the last hour, Catie has watched her kitten, Cottonball, climb up and down a tree. Now Cottonball is stuck in the branches, and Catie can't reach her!

Catie decides to call the local rescue squad. The squad tells her that they have a new set of ladders made by the Built-for-Branches Ladder Company. The special tree-climbing ladders are built in the following branch heights: 20 branches, 25 branches, 30 branches, 35 branches, and 40 branches.

To choose the best ladder for the job, the rescue squad asks Catie to find out the exact height of the tree in branches.

Luckily, Catie has been following Cottonball's pattern of climbing up and down the tree. From the bottom of the tree, Cottonball climbed up 7 branches and then down 4 branches. On her second move, she climbed up 5 branches and then down 2 branches. On her third move, she climbed up 7 branches and then down 4 branches. On her fourth move, she climbed up 5 branches and then down 2 branches. Cottonball reached the top branch during her tenth and final move.

Now It's Your Turn
Use Cottonball's pattern of climbing up and down the tree to help Catie figure out the tree's height in branches. Then tell which ladder the rescue squad should bring.

Bonus Box: Cottonball followed the same pattern above in a much taller tree. Draw a diagram or a table to show her position after each move. Follow the pattern to predict her position after the 17th move.

Shapely Nailing

Problem-solving strategies
students could use:
- draw a picture
- guess and check

Math skills
students will use:
- divide equally
- write equations
- add

Restating the problem: Mr. Saw, the shop teacher, assigned his students a project. Each group needed to nail three metal shapes—square, triangle, and pentagon—onto a wooden board using 96 nails. If the students used the same number of nails on each side of every shape, how many nails were used for each shape?

Important information found in the problem:
- Each group had to nail a square, a triangle, and a pentagon onto a board.
- Each group had 96 nails.
- The sides of every shape had to have the same number of nails.
- The corners of the shapes could not have nails.

Answer Key The square used 32 nails. The triangle used 24 nails. The pentagon used 40 nails.
(96 ÷ 12 total sides = 8 nails for each side.)
(8 x 4 sides of the square = 32.)
(8 x 3 sides of the triangle = 24.)
(8 x 5 sides of the pentagon = 40.)

Bonus Box answer: The square used 48 nails (96 ÷ 2 = 48). The triangle used 18 nails; the pentagon used 30 nails. (The triangle and the pentagon have 8 sides all together. 48 ÷ 8 = 6 nails per side. 6 x 3 sides = 18 nails for the triangle. 6 x 5 sides = 30 nails for the pentagon.)

Helpful Hints
Share this information when students get stuck to help put them back on the path to correctly solving the problem.

Hint 1 Draw a picture of each shape. How many sides does each shape have? *(square—4, triangle—3, pentagon—5)*

Hint 2 Draw a nail on each side of each shape. How many nails have you used? *(12)*

Hint 3 Continue placing nails, one on each side, until they all have been used.

Shapely Nailing

The math teachers at Mathland Elementary School wanted a new way to display geometry shapes. They were tired of making the shapes out of paper.

Mrs. Jones, one of the math teachers, went to Mr. Saw and explained the problem. Mr. Saw, the shop teacher, suggested that he could have the students make some cool metallic shapes. "The kids will really like the shiny shapes," he said.

Mrs. Jones was thrilled. She couldn't wait to see the new displays!

The next day, Mr. Saw presented his students with their projects. He gave each student group a long wooden board, plus a square, triangle, and pentagon cut from metal. Then Mr. Saw handed each group a cup filled with 96 nails. He directed the students in each group to nail the shapes onto the board, making sure each side had the same number of nails. He also added, "No nails in any of the shapes' corners."

With hammers in hand, the students got to work. The room was quickly filled with the sound of pounding hammers!

 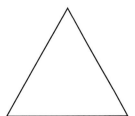 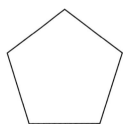

Now It's Your Turn
If each side had the same number of nails, how many nails were used for each shape?

Bonus Box: If the square had $\frac{1}{2}$ of the nails and the other two shapes combined had the other half, how many nails would be on each side of the triangle and the pentagon?

Seventh-Inning Snacks

Making a table to organize information

Teacher Page

Problem-solving strategies
students could use:

- make a table
- find a pattern

Math skills
students will use:

- skip-count by threes, fours, and sixes

Restating the problem: Lucy offered free snacks to every third, fourth, and sixth customer. How many customers received each combination of free snacks?

Important information found in the problem:
- Lucy gave every third customer a free drink.
- She gave every fourth customer a free popcorn.
- She gave every sixth customer a free pretzel.
- There were 24 customers in all.

Answer Key

Free Snacks	Number of Customers
Drink only	4
Popcorn only	4
Pretzel only	0
Drink and pretzel only	2
Drink, popcorn, and pretzel	2

Note: See table below.

Bonus Box answer: Only 1 customer would have received all 3 snacks for free. (The 24th customer would have received the other 3-snack combination.)

Helpful Hints

Share this information when students get stuck to help put them back on the path to correctly solving the problem.

Hint 1 How can you keep track of which snack each customer received? *(Make a table.)*

Hint 2 Make a table for the first 12 customers. What snack combinations do you notice? *(The sixth customer received a free drink and pretzel. The 12th customer received all 3 snacks.)*

Hint 3 How many customers received only a free pretzel? Explain why this happened. *(None. Every sixth customer received a free pretzel, but every third customer received a free drink. Since 6 is a multiple of 3, the sixth customer received a free drink along with the pretzel.)*

Hint 4 Predict what will happen to the data for customers 13–24. *(The data for customers 1–12 will repeat.)*

Customer	1	2	3	4	5	6	7	8	9	10	11	12	13	14	15	16	17	18	19	20	21	22	23	24
Free Drink			X			X			X			X			X			X			X			X
Free Popcorn				X				X				X				X				X				X
Free Pretzel						X						X						X						X

Seventh-Inning Snacks

Welcome to Lucy's Little League snack stand! Lucy sells drinks, popcorn, pretzels, peanuts, and hot dogs at local baseball games.

During a championship game, Lucy decided to offer a free giveaway to her customers after the seventh inning. She gave every third customer a free drink. She gave every fourth customer a free popcorn. She gave every sixth customer a free pretzel. Business was better than ever. Lucy counted 24 customers in all!

At the end of the game, Lucy wanted to record how many customers had received each combination of free snacks. However, she had forgotten to keep track of how many of each snack she had given to her customers!

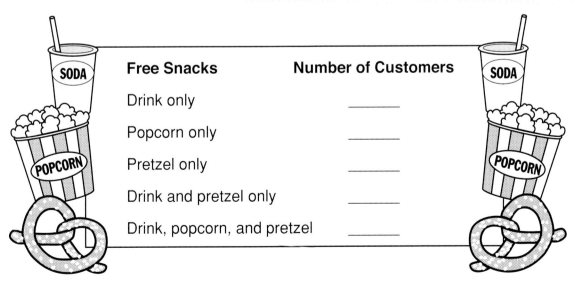

Free Snacks	Number of Customers
Drink only	_____
Popcorn only	_____
Pretzel only	_____
Drink and pretzel only	_____
Drink, popcorn, and pretzel	_____

Now It's Your Turn

Help Lucy record the information above by making a table. Use the information in the story to help you.

Bonus Box: How would the results have been different if only 23 customers had visited Lucy's snack stand?

A Garden-Variety Problem

Comparing two sales and choosing the better deal

Problem-solving strategies
students could use:

- find a pattern
- choose an operation

Math skills
students will use:

- add, subtract, and multiply
- skip-count decimals
- compare prices

Restating the problem: Two flower shops advertised sales. Cassie wanted to buy ten flowers for the lower cost. At which store should Cassie shop to get the better deal?

Important information found in the problem:
- Cassie wanted to buy ten flowers.
- Friendly Farms advertised four flowers for $1.25 each, with the fifth one free.
- Gentle Gardens advertised $1.50 for the first flower, $1.40 for the second flower, $1.30 for the third flower, and so on, with a limit of 15 flowers.

Answer Key Cassie will save $0.50 at Friendly Farms. At Friendly Farms, every fifth flower is free, so Cassie pays $10.00 for eight flowers ($1.25 x 8 = $10.00) and receives two free ones. At Gentle Gardens, Cassie will pay $10.50 for ten flowers ($1.50 + $1.40 + $1.30 + $1.20 + $1.10 + $1.00 + $0.90 + $0.80 + $0.70 + $0.60 = $10.50).

Bonus Box answer: Cassie will save $3.00 at Gentle Gardens. The flowers will cost $12.00 at Gentle Gardens. ($1.50 + $1.40 + $1.30 + $1.20 + $1.10 + $1.00 + $0.90 + $0.80 + $0.70 + $0.60 + $0.50 + $0.40 + $0.30 + $0.20 + $0.10 = $12.00). The flowers will cost $15.00 at Friendly Farms. Every fifth flower is free, so Cassie must pay for 12 flowers (12 x $1.25 = $15.00).

Helpful Hints

Share this information when students get stuck to help put them back on the path to correctly solving the problem.

Hint 1 At Friendly Farms, how many flowers will be received in all if four are purchased? *(5)* How many free flowers will Cassie receive if she buys ten flowers? *(2)* How many flowers will she need to purchase? *(8)*

Hint 2 Look at the deal offered by Gentle Gardens. Describe the pattern. *(The price for each additional flower is $0.10 less.)*

A Garden-Variety Problem

POW! #6

Cassie is a bargain hunter. Her friends call her the Queen of Consumers. If there's a sale, she's there!

Cassie decided to buy 10 flowers to plant in her garden, and she searched the newspaper for sales.

Friendly Farms advertised 4 flowers for $1.25, with the fifth one free. Gentle Gardens had a different offer: $1.50 for the first flower, $1.40 for the second flower, $1.30 for the third flower, and so on, with a limit of 15 flowers.

Cassie had a decision to make. From which store should she buy her flowers? If she took too long to decide, she'd miss out on the freshest ones. But if she didn't plan carefully, she'd miss out on the best buy!

Now It's Your Turn
Should Cassie shop at Friendly Farms or Gentle Gardens? Remember to find the better deal for buying 10 flowers. Then figure out how much Cassie will save.

Bonus Box: At which market should Cassie shop if she needs 15 flowers? Explain why.

Snail Trail

Using a pattern to determine how long it took a snail to climb a fence

Teacher Page

Problem-solving strategies students could use:

- draw a diagram
- guess and check
- look for a pattern

Math skills students will use:

- add and subtract
- look for a pattern

Restating the problem: Helen wanted to see how long it would take a snail to climb a 48-inch fence. The snail climbed six inches every day and slid back three inches every night. How many days did it take the snail to get to the top of the fence?

Important information found in the problem:
- The fence was 48 inches high.
- The snail began at the bottom of the fence.
- The snail climbed six inches up the fence every day.
- It slid three inches down the fence every night.

Answer Key It took the snail 15 days to reach the top of the fence. Written explanations will vary. On the first day, the snail climbed up 6 inches and slid back down 3 inches. On the second day, the snail began 3 inches from where it had started. The snail gained 3 inches every day. However, on the 15th day, the snail began 6 inches away from the top of the fence, so he reached the top by the end of the day.

Bonus Box answer: 17 days

Helpful Hints

Share this information when students get stuck to help put them back on the path to correctly solving the problem.

Hint 1 How far did the snail have to climb? *(48 inches)*

Hint 2 How many inches did the snail gain each day? *(3 inches)*

Hint 2 Try drawing a diagram to visualize the snail's travels.

Hint 2 Did the snail slide back on the last day? Why not? *(No, because he reached the top of the fence. The snail gained 6 inches on the last day.)*

Snail Trail

POW! #7

Helen loves helping her mom in the garden. She enjoys watering the flowers and watching the insects climb up and down the stems.

One day, Helen noticed a beautiful snail climbing up the fence. In fact, she continued to watch it until it was time to go inside.

The next day when Helen returned to the garden, the snail was still there, just a few inches past where it had been. Helen wondered how long it would take the snail to climb the entire height of the 48-inch fence. So she decided to find out.

Carefully, Helen removed the snail and placed it at the very bottom of the fence. Immediately, the snail began to climb. Helen measured the snail's distance right before she went inside for the day. She found that it had climbed 6 inches.

The next morning, Helen raced out to see the snail's progress. Surprisingly, she discovered that the snail had slid down 3 inches during the night. Helen loved the snail so much that she continued to watch its daily progress until it finally reached the top of the fence.

Now It's Your Turn

The snail climbed 6 inches up the fence each day and slid down 3 inches each night. How many days did it take the snail to reach the top of the fence?

Bonus Box: How many days would it take the snail to reach the top of a 54-inch fence?

Dog Show Daze

Creating a schedule and calculating elapsed time

Problem-solving strategies

students could use:
- guess and check
- work backward

Math skills

students will use:
- calculate elapsed time

Restating the problem: Penelope judges a dog every 25 minutes. Barney judges a dog every 45 minutes. Plan a schedule so that the judges start and finish at the same time, judge all 19 dogs, and take at least a 45-minute lunch break.

Important information found in the problem:
- The judges must judge 19 dogs.
- Penelope can judge one dog every 25 minutes.
- Barney can judge one dog every 45 minutes.
- The judging must begin at 10:00 A.M. and end exactly at 4:00 P.M.
- The judges must have at least 45 minutes for lunch, beginning sometime between 12:00 noon and 12:30 P.M.
- Lunch should be the judges' only break in the schedule.

Answer Key

Penelope's Schedule		Barney's Schedule	
1.	10:00 A.M.	1.	10:00 A.M.
2.	10:25 A.M.	2.	10:45 A.M.
3.	10:50 A.M.	3.	11:30 A.M.
4.	11:15 A.M.	Lunch	12:15 P.M.
5.	11:40 A.M.	4.	1:00 P.M.
Lunch	12:05 P.M.	5.	1:45 P.M.
6.	1:05 P.M.	6.	2:30 P.M.
7.	1:30 P.M.	7.	3:15 P.M.
8.	1:55 P.M.	Finish	4:00 P.M.
9.	2:20 P.M.		
10.	2:45 P.M.		
11.	3:10 P.M.		
12.	3:35 P.M.		
Finish	4:00 P.M.		

Bonus Box answer: beagle—11 points, poodle—9 points

Helpful Hints

Share this information when students get stuck to help put them back on the path to correctly solving the problem. If desired, provide each student with a manipulative clock to help with calculating elapsed time.

Hint 1 If the judging begins at 10:00 A.M., when will Penelope finish judging the first dog? *(10:25 A.M.)*

Hint 2 If the judging ends precisely at 4:00 P.M., what time should Penelope start judging the last dog? *(3:35 P.M.)*

Hint 3 List Penelope's schedule until you get close to lunchtime. What should you do next to make sure she ends exactly at 4:00 P.M.? *(Start making the schedule backward from 4:00 P.M.)*

Hint 4 Repeat this process to create Barney's schedule.

Dog Show Daze

Welcome to the annual Daybridge Dog Show!

Donna and Doug Doogal, the planners of the event, need to create a schedule for the show.

Penelope Pupperdink and Barney Milckbone are responsible for judging all 19 dogs. Each dog is judged by either Penelope or Barney.

Penelope will judge 1 dog every 25 minutes. Barney is a bit slower and will judge 1 dog every 45 minutes. The judging must begin at 10:00 A.M. and end exactly at 4:00 P.M. The judges must also stop for lunch sometime between 12:00 noon and 12:30 P.M. for at least 45 minutes. This should be the only break in their schedule.

It's the day before the dog show, and Donna and Doug are trying to make a schedule for the judges. After several hours, they are as dazed as ever. How will they ever schedule the day so that both judges start and finish at the same time?

If the Doogals don't figure it out, they'll end up in the doghouse!

Now It's Your Turn

Make a schedule for the judges that will include time to judge all 19 dogs. List the starting time that each dog will be judged. Be sure to include a lunch break.

Bonus Box: The 3 winners of the dog show all earned points toward their championship. The greyhound has 4 more points than the beagle. The beagle has 2 more points than the poodle. If the greyhound has 15 points, how many points do each of the other dogs have?

Checkered Gumballs

Determining wins, losses, and ties of checkers matches

Teacher Page

POW! #9

Problem-solving strategies
students could use:

- make an organized list
- guess and check
- make a table
- draw a picture

Math skills
students will use:

- visual diagrams
- addition
- logical reasoning

Restating the problem: Steven and John played matches of checkers. The winner of each match won five gumballs. For each tied match, the boys received one gumball each. If John received 31 gumballs, ten more than Steven, how many matches did each boy win? How many matches were ties?

Important information found in the problem:

- The boys played checkers every day for two weeks, or 14 days.
- A match was two games.
- A match winner received five gumballs.
- When a match ended in a tie, each boy received one gumball.
- John won 31 gumballs.
- John won ten more gumballs than Steven.

Answer Key John won 5 matches. Steven won 3 matches. Six matches were ties.
Written answers may vary. If 6 matches were ties, each boy would get 6 gumballs.
John had 31 gumballs. 31 − 6 = 25;
25 ÷ 5 gumballs = 5 matches won.
Steven had ten fewer gumballs. 31 − 10 = 21;
21 − 6 = 15; 15 ÷ 5 gumballs = 3 matches won.
5 + 3 + 6 = 14 matches played.

Bonus Box answer:
John—36 gumballs, Steven—24 gumballs
John: 5 matches won x 6 = 30; 30 + 6 = 36
Steven: 3 matches won x 6 = 18; 18 + 6 = 24

Helpful Hints

Share this information when students get stuck to help put them back on the path to correctly solving the problem.

Hint 1 Think about what's given in the problem. How many gumballs does John have? *(31)* How many gumballs does Steven have? *(He has 10 fewer than John, or 21.)* How many gumballs would each boy get for a tie? *(1)* How many for a win? *(5)*

Hint 2 How many days did they play? *(14)* Make an organized list or table with 14 spaces, one for each day the boys played.

Hint 3 Now, begin to fill in the table. What is the most number of matches John could win? *(6, because 31 ÷ 5 = 6, with 1 left over.)* What is the most number of matches Steven could win? *(4, because 21 ÷ 5 = 4, with 1 left over.)*

Hint 4 Could John have won six matches and Steven four matches? *(No, because that would mean there was only 1 tie. 6 + 4 + 1 = 11 days of matches. The boys played for 14 days.)*

Hint 5 Try again. Remember the boys played 14 days. When you add the number of matches John and Steven won together and the number of ties, the sum must equal 14.

Checkered Gumballs

John loved the summer. His cousin, Steven, always came to visit. This year, Steven was staying for two weeks!

On the day Steven arrived, John's mom suggested that the boys hold a checkers contest during Steven's visit. She told them that they could play a match, which was 2 games of checkers, each day. John's mom said that she would give the winner of a match 5 gumballs. If a match ended in a tie, she would give each boy 1 gumball. The boys loved the idea and began playing at once!

Each day the boys played checkers and turned in their results to John's mom. She kept a record of how many gumballs each boy would get. Finally, after the last match, John's mom tallied the results and gave each boy a bag of checkered gumballs.

John and Steven sat down to count their winnings. John was thrilled because he won 31 gumballs—10 more than Steven! Steven just grinned, popped a gumball in his mouth, and said, "I'll get you next year!"

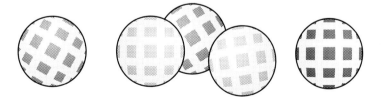

Now It's Your Turn
How many matches did each boy win? How many matches were ties?

Bonus Box: If John's mom awarded 6 gumballs instead of 5 for winning a match, how many gumballs would each boy have received?

Crash the Cans

Rearranging objects in a given number of moves

Problem-solving strategies

students could use:

- act it out
- guess and check

Math skills

students will use:

- spatial sense
- represent and visualize figures

Restating the problem: Ten cans are set up like bowling pins. Move three cans to reverse the arrangement.

Important information found in the problem:

- The ten cans are lined up so that one can is in the front row, two are in the next row, three are in the next row, and four are in the back row.
- The order of the rows must be reversed so that there are four cans in the front row, three in the next row, two in the next row, and one in the back row.
- The arrangement must be changed by moving only three cans.

Answer Key

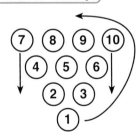

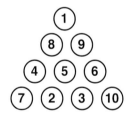

Bonus Box answer: Answers may vary. Can 5 should be positioned at the peak. The order of the remaining numbers in each row may vary. The sum of the numbers in each row should equal 25. One possible solution is shown.

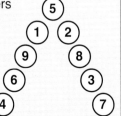

Helpful Hints

Share this information when students get stuck to help put them back on the path to correctly solving the problem. Have students use ten counters or other manipulatives to act out the problem.

Hint 1 Arrange your counters on a sheet of paper to show the first group of cans. Label the bottom row "front" and the top row "back."

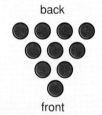

Hint 2 Draw the reversed group of cans beside the counters.

Hint 3 Study your drawing. Move the single counter so that it's behind the back row.

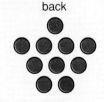

Hint 4 Compare the counters with your drawing. Which two rows are the same? *(first and third)* Which two rows need to be changed? *(second and fourth)*

Hint 5 Move two more counters so that your arrangement matches your drawing.

Crash the Cans

The kids in Kenny's neighborhood like to play Crash the Cans.

They line up 10 cans so that 1 can is in the front row, 2 are in the next row, 3 are in the next row, and 4 are in the back row. Then they roll a tennis ball to knock them over.

One day, Kenny challenged his friend Kevin to reverse the group of cans so that there would be 4 cans in the front row, 3 in the next row, 2 in the next row, and 1 in the back row.

Kenny told Kevin to reverse the group by moving just 3 cans.

Now It's Your Turn
Help Kevin reverse the group of cans. Remember that you can move only 3 cans.

Bonus Box: Number the cans on the right 1–9 so that the sum of each row equals 25.

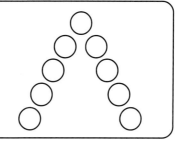

Decisions, Decisions!

Determining combinations of activities

Teacher Page

Problem-solving strategies
students could use:
- work backward
- guess and check

Math skills
students will use:
- write an equation
- add money amounts
- solve for missing addends
- add and subtract

Welcome to Eli's!
Today's Activities
Mini Golf—6 tokens
Bowling—4 tokens
Go-Carts—8 tokens
Batting Cages—3 tokens
Table Tennis—5 tokens
Movie Room—7 tokens
Video Games—1 token per game
1 token = $0.75

Restating the problem: The three girls needed to decide how to spend the afternoon at Eli's Entertainment Center. Given the number of tokens purchased with $10.50, what four different activities did the girls select?

Important information found in the problem:
- Ellen had $10.50.
- Each token at Eli's was $0.75.
- Ellen and her friends wanted to participate in four different activities.
- They didn't want to have any tokens left over.

Answer Key The girls bought 14 tokens each with $10.50. ($10.50 ÷ $0.75 = 14) They played mini golf, bowled, visited the batting cages, and played 1 video game. (6 + 4 + 3 + 1 = 14)

Bonus Box answer: Ellen could have gotten 18 tokens.
($10.50 − $6.00 = $4.50; $4.50 ÷ $0.75 = 6;
   12 + 6 = 18 tokens)
She saved $3.00. ($10.50 − $6.00 = $4.50;
   $0.75 x 2 = 1.50; $4.50 − $1.50 = $3.00 saved)

Helpful Hints
Share this information when students get stuck to help put them back on the path to correctly solving the problem.

Hint 1 Think about how much money each girl had to spend. Then determine how many tokens she could have purchased with that amount *(14 tokens)*. Use manipulatives or subtract the token value from $10.50.

Hint 2 Think about the activities they could have done with 14 tokens. Try to guess and check to get a total of 14.

Hint 3 Remember that the girls wanted to participate in four different activities.

Hint 4 Try to find combinations of three activities that equal ten tokens. If four tokens are left over, what other activity could the girls have done?

Decisions, Decisions!

Welcome to Eli's!
Today's Activities
Mini Golf—6 tokens
Bowling—4 tokens
Go-Carts—8 tokens
Batting Cages—3 tokens
Table Tennis—5 tokens
Movie Room—7 tokens
Video Games—1 token per game

1 token = $0.75

In Ellen's mind, her mom couldn't drive fast enough! Ellen was on her way to meet her two best friends at Eli's Entertainment Center. Everyone knew that Eli's was the best place to spend a Saturday afternoon.

When they arrived, Ellen's mom gave her $10.50 to spend. She told Ellen that she'd be back in three hours to pick her up. Ellen knew she'd be able to do a lot because activity tokens were only $0.75 each. Smiling, she bounded out of the car to meet her friends.

Ellen raced to the token counter. After she bought her tokens, she joined her friends, Christy and Ann, in front of the activity board. The girls were looking at the list and trying to decide what to do. Each girl, including Ellen, had the same number of tokens to use. They each wanted to use all of their tokens. Finally, the trio agreed on 4 activities. Decisions made, the girls began a fun-filled afternoon at Eli's!

Now It's Your Turn
Look at the activity board from Eli's Entertainment Center. Which 4 activities did the girls select?

Bonus Box: Eli was running a special on tokens. He was selling the first dozen for $6.00. Each additional token cost $0.75 each. How many tokens could Ellen have gotten with her $10.50? How much would she have saved if she bought the same number of tokens as in the problem above?

Geometric Granny

Finding the perimeter and area of a rectangle

Teacher Page

Problem-solving strategies

students could use:
- draw a picture
- work backward
- find a pattern

Math skills

students will use:
- add, subtract, and multiply whole numbers
- write number sentences
- find perimeter and area

Restating the problem: Granny knitted an afghan with a green rectangle in the center and six three-inch-wide frames. If the afghan is 42 inches wide and 54 inches long, what is the perimeter and area of the green rectangle?

Important information found in the problem:
- Granny started with a green rectangle.
- Granny added frames in the following colors and order: yellow, orange, red, purple, white, and blue.
- The afghan is 42 inches wide and 54 inches long.
- Each frame is three inches wide.
- Georgia must find the perimeter and the area of the green rectangle.

Answer Key The perimeter of the green rectangle is 48 inches. The area is 108 square inches. The rectangle is 6 inches wide (42 − 6 x 6 = 6) and 18 inches long (54 − 6 x 6 = 18).

Bonus Box answer: The area of the blue frame is 540 square inches.

Helpful Hints

Share this information when students get stuck to help put them back on the path to correctly solving the problem.

Hint 1 How many frames did Granny knit around the green rectangle? *(6)*

Hint 2 What is the width and length of the afghan? Label each side. *(42 inches and 54 inches)*

Hint 3 Look at the rectangle enclosed by the outer frame. How much smaller is the smaller rectangle's width and length than the larger rectangle? *(6 inches)* How do you know? *(The frame is 3 inches wide on each side.)*

Hint 4 What pattern can you follow to find the width and length of the green rectangle? *(subtract 6 six times)*

Geometric Granny

Georgia's granny is one cool lady. She crochets, knits, and even in-line skates! Granny is also a geometric genius.

When Georgia asked her grandmother to knit her an afghan, Granny got a gleam in her eye. Georgia could almost see the needles turning in her head. Then Granny said, "I'll make you an awesome afghan—a Granny specialty—only if you agree to solve a geometric riddle when it's done."

Georgia accepted the challenge.

For the next few months, Granny rocked, rolled, and knitted. The afghan was coming together beautifully. Granny started with a green rectangle. Then she added a yellow frame around it. Next came an orange frame. Georgia got really excited when Granny added a red, a purple, a white, and then a blue frame, in that order. Finally, the afghan was finished. Granny was right—it was awesome!

Granny told Georgia proudly, "Your afghan is 42 inches wide and 54 inches long. Each frame is 3 inches wide." As Georgia reached for the afghan, Granny playfully pulled it away. "You still have a riddle to solve, young lady. Without using a ruler, find the perimeter and the area of the green rectangle."

Georgia studied the afghan and scratched her head. She sketched and calculated until her brain was sore. Granny watched Georgia with a smile, knowing that her clever granddaughter would find the solution.

Now It's Your Turn
Find the answer to Granny's riddle. Figure out the area and perimeter of the green rectangle.

Bonus Box: Find the area of the outer blue frame. (Hint: Try to find four rectangles within the frame.)

Fishing for Answers

Working backward to find the number of sea creatures

Problem-solving strategies
students could use:
- work backward
- make an organized list
- draw a picture
- guess and check
- use logical reasoning

Math skills
students will use:
- add and subtract
- multiply and divide

Restating the problem: Someone disturbed Seamore C. Life's food order. In its place was a riddle. Use the riddle to determine how many sea creatures are in the aquarium.

Important information found in the problem:
- There are 25 crabs.
- There are nine more crabs than eels.
- There are half as many sharks as eels.
- There are six fewer sharks than jellyfish.
- There are three times as many starfish as sharks.
- There are twice as many angelfish as starfish.

Answer Key There are 135 sea creatures. There are 25 crabs, 16 eels (25 crabs − 9 = 16), 8 sharks (16 eels ÷ 2 = 8), 14 jellyfish (8 sharks + 6 = 14), 24 starfish (8 sharks x 3 = 24), and 48 angelfish (24 starfish x 2 = 48).

Bonus Box answer:
Seamore will order 391 pounds of food:
- 25 crabs x 3 pounds = 75
- 16 eels x 5 pounds = 80
- 8 sharks x 5 pounds = 40
- 14 jellyfish x 2 pounds = 28
- 24 starfish x 3 pounds = 72
- 48 angelfish x 2 pounds = 96

75 + 80 + 40 + 28 + 72 + 96 = 391 pounds of food.

Helpful Hints
Share this information when students get stuck to help put them back on the path to correctly solving the problem.

Hint 1 Start with the last line of the riddle and work backward.

Hint 2 You know the number of which sea creature? *(crab)* How many are there? *(25)*

Hint 3 If there are 25 crabs, how many eels are there? *(16, because there are 9 more crabs than eels; 25 − 9 = 16)*

Hint 4 Now that you know the number of eels, how do you figure out the number of sharks? *(Divide the number of eels by 2.)*

Hint 5 How can you figure out the number of jellyfish? *(Add 6 to the number of sharks.)*

Hint 6 How can you figure out the number of starfish? *(Multiply the number of sharks by 3.)*

Hint 7 What will you do to figure out the number of angelfish? *(Multiply the number of starfish by 2.)*

Fishing for Answers

POW! #13

Something fishy happened at the local aquarium.

The police received a call from Seamore C. Life, the aquarium manager. Seamore stated that the office was a wreck and that someone had mixed up all the order forms. He was worried most about the food order. He knew supplies were running low for all of the aquarium's creatures. Seamore also reported that when he finally found the food order form, his order had been erased. In its place was this riddle:

Twice as many angelfish as starfish
    swim around the tank.
Three times as many starfish as sharks
    hover by the bank.
Six fewer sharks than jellyfish
    hunt for their prey.
Half as many sharks as eels
    play all day.
Nine more crabs than eels
    swim by the shore.
Watching 25 crabs
    will never be a bore!

If this was someone's idea of a joke, Seamore does not find it very funny. He is trying to solve the riddle so that his food order can be placed on time.

If you have any information about this incident, please notify the police.

Now It's Your Turn
Help Seamore figure out the total number of creatures at the aquarium.

Bonus Box: Seamore needs to order 2 pounds of food for each angelfish and jellyfish, 3 pounds for each starfish and crab, and 5 pounds for each eel and shark. How many pounds of food will Seamore order in all?

What's the Scoop?

Using an organized list to find ice-cream combinations

Problem-solving strategies
students could use:
- make an organized list, table, or chart
- look for patterns
- logical reasoning

Math skills
students will use:
- account for all possibilities
- make a list
- identify, extend, and use patterns

Restating the problem: Will, Jill, and Phil are trying to determine all the possible triple-scoop cone combinations they can make using vanilla, chocolate chip, and strawberry ice cream.

Important information found in the problem:
- There are three different flavors of ice cream.
- Each cone has three scoops.
- The flavors can be in any order.
- Flavors can be repeated on the cone.
- Flavors can be reversed.

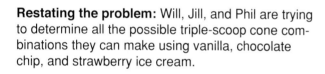 There are 27 different combinations. V = vanilla, C = chocolate chip, S = strawberry
VVV, VVC, VCV, VCC, VVS, VSV, VSS, VCS, VSC
CCC, CCS, CSC, CSS, CCV, CVC, CVV, CVS, CSV
SSS, SSV, SVS, SVV, SSC, SCS, SCC, SCV, SVC

Bonus Box answer:
There are 9 different combinations.
C = cookie dough, M = mint, B = bubble gum
    CC, CM, CB
    MM, MC, MB
    BB, BC, BM

Helpful Hints

Share this information when students get stuck to help put them back on the path to correctly solving the problem.

Hint 1 Is it possible to have a cone with just one flavor? *(Yes, there are three possible combinations: all chocolate chip, all vanilla, and all strawberry.)*

Hint 2 Think about the two-scoop combinations. How were the combinations with two different flavors arranged? *(The vanilla came first on one cone, and the chocolate chip came first on the other cone. The order was flipped.)*

Hint 3 How could you make an organized list? Try listing all the combinations with vanilla in the first position.

Hint 4 Now try listing all the combinations with chocolate chip in the first position. Then try it with strawberry in the first position.

Hint 5 Do you notice a pattern? How many combinations were there with a two-scoop cone of two flavor choices? *(2 x 2 = 4)* How many combinations do you think there will be with a triple-scoop cone of three flavor choices? *(3 x 3 x 3 = 27)*

What's the Scoop?

Will, Jill, and Phil are triplets. They are meeting at the Tasty Treats Ice-Cream Shop for an afternoon snack. Will and Jill arrive together, but their brother isn't there yet. While they are waiting for Phil, Will and Jill wonder how many different double-scoop ice-cream cone combinations they can make with their two favorite flavors, chocolate chip and vanilla.

Will, who likes only vanilla, says, "One combination would be to have two scoops of vanilla."

Jill replies, "Another cone could have two scoops of chocolate chip since that is my favorite."

The lady behind the counter adds, "You could always put vanilla on the bottom and chocolate chip on top."

"Or you could turn the order around and have chocolate chip on the bottom and vanilla on top!" declares Jill.

"Wow! We could have four different combinations using our two favorite flavors," concludes Will.

Just then Phil arrives and joins them at the counter. When he asks what they are doing, Will and Jill tell him how they can make four different cone combinations using their two favorite ice-cream flavors.

Phil thinks for a moment and states, "I wonder how many different triple-scoop cones we could make if we added my favorite flavor, strawberry."

"Let's find out!" exclaim Jill and Will in unison.

Now It's Your Turn
Help the triplets figure out how many different triple-scoop combinations they can make using vanilla, chocolate chip, and strawberry ice cream.

Bonus Box: How many combinations would there be if the triplets ordered double-scoop cones, but chose from cookie dough, mint, and bubble gum ice cream?

King Garther's Royal Room

Computing all the possible dimensions of a rectangle with a given perimeter

Problem-solving strategies

students could use:

- write an equation
- draw a picture
- make an organized list

Math skills

students will use:

- calculate perimeter and area
- determine dimensions for a given perimeter
- add and multiply

Restating the problem: Help the builders find the dimensions for a room that has a perimeter of 48 meters and will require the most square tiles whose sides are one meter.

Important information found in the problem:

- The room must be rectangular.
- The room must have a perimeter of 48 meters.
- The builders must list all the possible dimensions for the room.
- The floor must require as many square tiles with one-meter sides as possible.

Answer Key The royal room should be 12 x 12 meters. The perimeter is 48 meters (12 + 12 + 12 + 12 = 48). The area is 144 square meters (12 x 12 = 144). These measurements will result in a floor that will require the most tiles. All possible dimensions for a room with a perimeter of 48 meters are listed below.

Dimensions	Area
23 x 1 meters	23 square meters
22 x 2 meters	44 square meters
21 x 3 meters	63 square meters
20 x 4 meters	80 square meters
19 x 5 meters	95 square meters
18 x 6 meters	108 square meters
17 x 7 meters	119 square meters
16 x 8 meters	128 square meters
15 x 9 meters	135 square meters
14 x 10 meters	140 square meters
13 x 11 meters	143 square meters
12 x 12 meters	144 square meters

Bonus Box answer: 48 gold tiles, 96 silver tiles

Helpful Hints

Share this information when students get stuck to help put them back on the path to correctly solving the problem.

Hint 1 Reread the information that describes the room. What do you know about the room that the builders need to design? *(It is rectangular. The perimeter must be 48 meters. The floor must require as many square tiles with one-meter sides as possible.)*

Hint 2 Think about the perimeter of the room. Draw a room and label the sides so that it matches the perimeter. List the dimensions. List a second set of dimensions. How can you organize your list so that you account for all possible dimensions? *(Begin by listing the smallest dimensions: 23 x 1.)*

Hint 3 Now that you have listed all of the possible dimensions for the room, consider which one is most fit for King Garther. The room should hold the most square tiles possible. To which type of measurement does this refer? *(area)*

King Garther's Royal Room

King Garther, the 48th king of the land of Perimelot, made a decree to add a new room to the castle.

He immediately summoned his royal builders to begin planning the project. He decreed that the room must be rectangular and have a perimeter of exactly 48 meters. The builders suggested gold and silver tile for the room's floor. The king was delighted by the idea!

The builders knew that their jolly king would be pleased with anything they designed. Yet their plans had to be approved by the queen, who made the final decorating decisions.

The builders remembered how much King Garther loved the idea of the gold and silver tiles. They decided to present the king and queen with a list of all the possible dimensions for the room. Then they would choose the room whose floor would require the most square tiles with one-meter sides.

The builders got to work immediately, prepared to toil throughout the night.

Now It's Your Turn
Help the builders design a room fit for a king! Remember to follow King Garther's instructions. Then choose the design that best matches the king's wishes.

Bonus Box: The builders decided to lay the tile in the following pattern: gold, silver, silver. How many gold tiles will they use? How many silver tiles?

Frames on Display

Using the guess-and-check strategy to fill a 5 x 5 grid

Teacher Page

Problem-solving strategies
students could use:

- make a diagram
- look for patterns
- logical reasoning
- guess and check
- look for a pattern

Math skills
students will use:

- visual diagrams

Restating the problem: Iris's dad wanted to set up an eyeglass display. He had 25 pairs of glasses: five each of silver, blue, black, brown, and gold. Iris needed to place them in a 5 x 5 grid, but she couldn't repeat a color in a row, column, or diagonal. What would Iris's display look like?

Important information found in the problem:
- Iris needed to place the glasses in a 5 x 5 grid.
- There were five pairs each of silver, blue, black, brown, and gold eyeglass frames.
- A frame color could not be repeated in a row, column, or diagonal.

Answer Key Answers may vary. The following is one possible solution.

silver	blue	brown	gold	black
gold	black	silver	blue	brown
blue	brown	gold	black	silver
black	silver	blue	brown	gold
brown	gold	black	silver	blue

Bonus Box answer: Answers may vary. The display will be a 7 x 7 grid. The following is one possible solution.

green	clear	hazel	blue	aqua	violet	brown
blue	aqua	violet	brown	green	clear	hazel
brown	green	clear	hazel	blue	aqua	violet
hazel	blue	aqua	violet	brown	green	clear
violet	brown	green	clear	hazel	blue	aqua
clear	hazel	blue	aqua	violet	brown	green
aqua	violet	brown	green	clear	hazel	blue

Helpful Hints

Share this information when students get stuck to help put them back on the path to correctly solving the problem.

Hint 1 How would the display look? *(a 5 x 5 grid)* Draw the grid.

Hint 2 What colors were the eyeglass frames that needed to be placed in the grid? *(silver, blue, black, brown, and gold)* How many frames of each color were there? *(5)*

Hint 3 Place one color in the grid first. Think about the rules for the grid. Where can't the same color frames go? *(in the same row, column, or diagonal)* Lightly mark an X in the squares that you can't put that color.

Hint 4 Double-check to be sure you're following the rules. Then put in the next five frames of a different color.

Hint 5 Do you notice a pattern? *(The order of the 5 colors is the same in each column. The colors shift down 3 spaces in each successive column.)*

Frames on Display

POW! #16

Iris loves eyes. For as long as she can remember, she has wanted to be an eye doctor, just like her dad. She can't wait to learn more about how the eye works!

One day when Iris was visiting her dad's office she overheard her dad talking to a salesman who sold eyeglasses. He was showing her dad the five different frame colors available—silver, blue, black, brown, and gold. Iris's dad agreed to sell the glasses in his office, but only if the frames were displayed in an eye-catching way.

Her dad suggested that 25 frames—five of each color—be displayed in a 5 x 5 grid. The only problem was that no color could be repeated in a row, column, or diagonal.

Since Iris also loves challenging puzzles, she decided to step in. She told the man that she would help him organize his display. He was so thrilled, they got started at once!

Now It's Your Turn
Help Iris and the salesman figure out one way that the eyeglass frames could be displayed.

Bonus Box: Iris's dad wanted to display pairs of contact lenses the same way he displays his eyeglasses. If he had seven pairs each of seven different types of lenses—green, blue, brown, hazel, violet, clear, and aqua—show how his display would have looked. Remember: A lens type cannot be repeated in a row, column, or diagonal.

A Dime a Dance

Determining the number of dance tickets purchased by two girls

Problem-solving strategies

students could use:

- guess and check
- work backward
- draw a picture
- write an equation

Math skills

students will use:

- add money
- divide
- multiply

Restating the problem: Susan and Tammy bought dance tickets for $0.10 each. They spent $4.40 combined. If Susan spent three times more than Tammy, how many tickets does Susan have? How many tickets do the girls have all together?

Important information found in the problem:
- The girls bought $4.40 worth of tickets all together.
- Each ticket cost $0.10.
- Susan spent three times more than Tammy.

Answer Key The girls bought 44 tickets together ($4.40 ÷ $0.10 = 44). Susan bought 33 tickets. Tammy bought 11 tickets.

Bonus Box answer: 2,540 tickets were sold ($254.00 ÷ $0.10 = 2,540).

Helpful Hints

Share this information when students get stuck to help put them back on the path to correctly solving the problem.

Hint 1 Think about how much money the girls spent. How much did each ticket cost? *($0.10)* How will you figure out how many tickets they purchased? *(Divide $0.10 into $4.40.)*

Hint 2 Make a guess for the number of Tammy's tickets. Multiply that number by three to get a number for Susan's tickets. Now add Tammy and Susan's tickets. Do they equal 44?

Hint 3 If your sum is smaller than 44, what do you need to do? *(Try a larger number for Tammy.)* If your sum is larger than 44, what do you need to do? *(Try a smaller number.)*

Hint 4 Keep guessing and checking until the sum of the two numbers equals 44.

A Dime a Dance

The principal of Jefferson Elementary School wanted to build a new gymnasium. In order to do that, the school needed to raise money. The students voted on how they could help raise funds. They decided to hold a school dance in the cafeteria.

Immediately, the students got to work decorating the cafeteria and printing tickets. The tickets would be sold for admission and dances. The students figured they could charge a dime for each dance to make more money for the new gym.

When the dance day arrived, music was blaring from the cafeteria. Everyone was having a great time. In the corner, Tammy and Susan were comparing dance tickets. Together, they spent $4.40. Susan spent three times more than Tammy. Tammy asked Susan how many tickets she had. Susan said that she had *a lot!*

As Susan raced off to the dance floor, Tammy sat down to figure out how many tickets Susan had purchased. Tammy soon knew Susan would be one tired girl by the end of the dance!

Now It's Your Turn
Help Tammy figure out how many tickets Susan bought. How many tickets did they have all together?

Bonus Box: All together the students raised $254.00 selling dance tickets. How many dance tickets were sold?

Coupon Clippers

Figuring out coupon discounts

Teacher Page

Problem-solving strategies
students could use:
- guess and check
- choose the correct operation

Math skills
students will use:
- add and subtract decimals
- estimate money

Restating the problem: Use the number of coupons Penny gave each friend, the value of each coupon, and the information on the receipts to determine which receipt belongs to whom.

Important information found in the problem:
- Penny gave three coupons to Collin, two coupons to Cody, and one coupon to Connie.
- The receipts show the regular price for each ingredient.
- Each receipt shows the total cost after redeeming the coupons: $10.74, $10.70, and $11.54.

Answer Key Cody spent $10.74, Collin spent $10.79, and Connie spent $11.54.

Bonus Box answer: Penny forgot the $0.30 sugar coupon. (The total regular cost of all the items is $11.79. Penny paid $9.79. She saved $2.00 by using coupons. The total value of all six coupons is $2.30, which means she did not use the $0.30 sugar coupon.)

Helpful Hints
Share this information when students get stuck to help put them back on the path to correctly solving the problem.

Hint 1 Look at the receipts. How are the receipts the same? *(They have the same items and prices.)* How do they differ? *(Each one shows a different total.)* How can you explain this difference? *(The friends saved different amounts of money because they used different coupons.)*

Hint 2 How can you find out how much each friend saved using coupons? *(Find the total regular cost of the items: $11.79. Then, for each receipt, subtract the total shown from the cost of the items: receipt 1—$1.05, receipt 2—$1.00, receipt 3—$0.25.)*

Hint 3 The story tells how many coupons each friend used. Look at the amount that each friend saved by using coupons. Which friend used only one coupon? *(Connie)* How do you know? *(She saved $0.25. This is the coupon for butter.)*

Hint 4 What strategy can you used to figure out which coupons the other two friends used? *(guess and check)*

Coupon Clippers

Penny Pincher is the chairperson of the bake sale at Morefunds Elementary School. She asked three of her friends to buy ingredients for cookies.

To save money, Penny searched the newspaper and found 2 coupons for each ingredient on her list. She kept one set of coupons for herself. Then she gave 3 coupons to Collin, 2 coupons to Cody, and 1 coupon to Connie. Penny promised to pay back her friends if they saved their receipts.

After Collin, Cody, and Connie went shopping, Penny collected their receipts. Later on, Penny realized that she forgot to write each person's name on his or her receipt! The receipts show the regular price for each ingredient. Each one also shows the total cost after redeeming the coupons.

Penny looked over the coupons that she saved for herself. They were the exact coupons that she had given her friends. She also remembered how many coupons she gave each person.

But how could she figure out which receipt belonged to whom? Penny threw up her hands in despair. If only she had paid more attention to math than baking!

Now It's Your Turn
Help Penny figure out which receipt belongs to each friend. Use the receipts and coupons above to help you.

Bonus Box: Penny bought each of the ingredients at the store and spent $9.79. She used all of her coupons except one. Which coupon did she forget?

Just Clowning Around

Using logical reasoning to create a schedule

Teacher Page

Problem-solving strategies
students could use:

- logical reasoning
- make an organized table

Math skills
students will use:

- order and sequence
- eliminate solutions
- evaluate clues

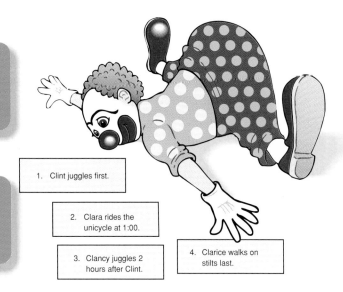

1. Clint juggles first.

2. Clara rides the unicycle at 1:00.

3. Clancy juggles 2 hours after Clint.

4. Clarice walks on stilts last.

Restating the problem: Five future clowns named Clara, Clint, Clancy, Clarice, and Clementine are learning five new clown skills: juggling, putting on makeup, riding a unicycle, performing magic tricks, and walking on stilts. Use the clues provided to help organize a schedule of their afternoon events.

Important information found in the problem:
- There are five campers: Clara, Clint, Clancy, Clarice, and Clementine.
- The activities take place every hour from 12:00 P.M. until 5:00 P.M.
- The clowns are learning five new activities: juggling, putting on makeup, riding a unicycle, performing magic tricks, and walking on stilts.

Answer Key

	Clara	Clint	Clancy	Clarice	Clementine
12:00–1:00	magic tricks	juggling	stilts	makeup	unicycle
1:00–2:00	unicycle	magic tricks	makeup	juggling	stilts
2:00–3:00	stilts	makeup	juggling	unicycle	magic tricks
3:00–4:00	juggling	stilts	unicycle	magic tricks	makeup
4:00–5:00	makeup	unicycle	magic tricks	stilts	juggling

Bonus Box answer: Answers will vary.

Helpful Hints

Share this information when students get stuck to help put them back on the path to correctly solving the problem.

Hint 1   Make a table to organize your information. Label the top of each column with a clown's name. Label each row with the time.

Hint 2   Read the first clue. What does it tell you? *(Clint will juggle first, which is at 12:00.)* Write "juggling" in your table in Clint's column and in the 12:00–1:00 row.

Hint 3   Read the next clue. Does it give you specific information? *(yes)* Record all the clues with specific information in your table.

Hint 4   Use reasoning to fill in other boxes. For example, if one row or column has all but one box filled, what does that tell you? *(The activity that has not been used in that row or column must go in the blank space.)*

Just Clowning Around

POW! #19

At Camp Clown-Around, future clowns spend their afternoons from 12:00 P.M. until 5:00 P.M. learning clown skills. This week, Clara, Clint, Clancy, Clarice, and Clementine are at camp. They practice juggling, putting on makeup, riding a unicycle, performing magic tricks, and walking on stilts. Every day, each clown spends an hour on each skill. No clowns do the same activity at the same time.

On the morning of the first day, Clifford, the camp director, announced the afternoon's schedule. The five campers were so excited! They ran out to meet Clifford by the schedule board. Unfortunately, none of the future clowns were watching where they were going. Before Clifford could say, "Watch out!" they crashed into the board and scattered the schedule cards everywhere.

"Oh, no!" exclaimed Clifford. "What are we going to do?"

"Never fear!" said Charlie, his secretary. I think I may have some clues that will help you!

Hoping the clues would help, the clowns-to-be got to work helping Clifford fix the schedule.

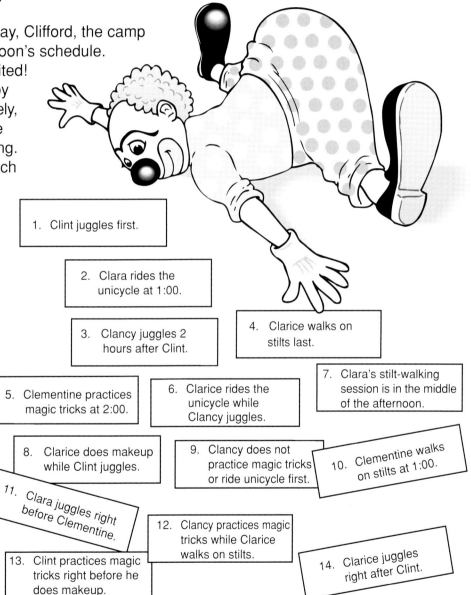

1. Clint juggles first.

2. Clara rides the unicycle at 1:00.

3. Clancy juggles 2 hours after Clint.

4. Clarice walks on stilts last.

7. Clara's stilt-walking session is in the middle of the afternoon.

5. Clementine practices magic tricks at 2:00.

6. Clarice rides the unicycle while Clancy juggles.

8. Clarice does makeup while Clint juggles.

9. Clancy does not practice magic tricks or ride unicycle first.

10. Clementine walks on stilts at 1:00.

11. Clara juggles right before Clementine.

12. Clancy practices magic tricks while Clarice walks on stilts.

13. Clint practices magic tricks right before he does makeup.

14. Clarice juggles right after Clint.

Now It's Your Turn
Help the 5 campers and Clifford use the clues to arrange the afternoon schedule.

Bonus Box: Ask 15 of your classmates which clown skill they'd most enjoy learning. Collect the data and display it on a bar graph.

A Penny a Day

Listing coin combinations from 1¢ to $1

Problem-solving strategies

students could use:
- make an organized list, table, or chart
- draw a picture
- look for patterns
- act it out

Math skills

students will use:
- identify patterns
- identify coins
- count coins
- show equivalent values of coins

Restating the problem: Jake receives a penny from his parents each day. He trades up for larger coins whenever he can until he gets a dollar. On which days will Jake have the most coins? What are those coins?

Important information found in the problem:
- Jake receives a penny each day.
- On the fifth day, Jake trades his pennies for a nickel.
- On the tenth day, Jake trades his nickel and five pennies for a dime.
- Jake trades for larger coins whenever possible.
- Jake trades for 100 days.

Answer Key   Written explanations may vary.
Jake will have 8 coins on days 94 and 99.
On day 94 he will have 1 half-dollar, 1 quarter, 1 dime, 1 nickel, and 4 pennies.
On day 99 he will have 1 half-dollar, 1 quarter, 2 dimes, and 4 pennies.

Bonus Box answer: Possible answers include the following:
   1 quarter, 1 penny
   2 dimes, 1 nickel, 1 penny
   2 dimes, 6 pennies
   1 dime, 3 nickels, 1 penny
   1 dime, 2 nickels, 6 pennies
   1 dime, 16 pennies
   5 nickels, 1 penny
   4 nickels, 6 pennies
   3 nickels, 11 pennies
   2 nickels, 16 pennies
   1 nickel, 21 pennies
   26 pennies

Helpful Hints

Share this information when students get stuck to help put them back on the path to correctly solving the problem.

Hint 1   List all the U.S. coins under one dollar. *(penny, nickel, dime, quarter, half-dollar).* What are the values of each coin? *(penny = 1¢, nickel = 5¢, dime = 10¢, quarter = 25¢, half-dollar = 50¢)*

Hint 2   How much does Jake receive on the first day? *(1¢)* How much does he receive on the second day? *(1¢)* How much does Jake have after two days? *(2¢)* How has his amount changed? *(It has gone up by one cent.)*

Hint 3   On day five, how much does Jake have? *(5¢)* Can he trade these coins for a larger coin? *(Yes, he can trade the five pennies for a nickel.)*

Hint 4   When is the next time Jake can trade? *(on day ten)* What will he trade for? *(He will trade his nickel and five pennies for a dime.)*

Hint 5   Keep going. Do you notice a pattern? *(Jake trades every five days.)*

A Penny a Day

Jake likes to trade things. He enjoys trading seats on the bus. He likes to trade lunches, erasers, lollipops, and just about everything else. In fact, when Jake grows up, he wants to trade on the stock market.

Right now, Jake's favorite things to trade are coins. That's because his parents give him a penny every day.

Now a penny isn't much of an allowance, but that doesn't bother Jake. He knows that in just 5 short days he gets to do his favorite thing—trade! Jake will trade his 5 pennies for a nickel. Then, on the 10th day, Jake will trade his nickel and 5 pennies for a dime. For Jake, there's nothing better than trading a handful of change. He trades his coins for larger coins, including quarters and half-dollars, every time he can.

Jake wants to keep collecting and trading until he trades for a crisp new dollar bill. Imagine all the trades he will make in 100 days!

Jake knows that each day he trades, he'll have fewer coins than the day before. Jake wonders on which days he'll have the most coins and what the coins will be. He has lots of time to figure it out, so he trades with his sister to get a pencil and notebook. Before long, Jake gets to work!

Now It's Your Turn
Help Jake figure out on which days he will have the most coins. Remember, he also wants to know what those coins are.

Bonus Box: Show Jake 10 different coin combinations for the amount of money that he will have on the 26th day.

Time for a Mystery

Calculating elapsed time

Problem-solving strategies
students could use:
- logical reasoning
- work backward

Math skills
students will use:
- calculate elapsed time

Restating the problem: Using the clues, figure out each guest's departure time. Then identify the guest who left at the same time the diamond was stolen.

Important information found in the problem:
- The jewel detector went off at 8:05 P.M.
- The detector went off when the thief left the museum.
- Sam Silver left one hour and 25 minutes before Opal Owen.
- Susie Sapphire left 90 minutes before Amelia Amethyst.
- Jeffrey Jade left 55 minutes after Sam Silver.
- Ruby Reynolds left at 7:50 P.M.
- Diamond Diaz left 15 minutes before Patty Pearl.
- Peter Platinum left 105 minutes before Garth Gold.
- Patty Pearl left 25 minutes before Jeffrey Jade.
- Opal Owen left two hours and 50 minutes after Ruby Reynolds.
- Garth Gold left 75 minutes after Susie Sapphire.
- Amelia Amethyst left 35 minutes after Diamond Diaz.

Helpful Hints
Share this information when students get stuck to help put them back on the path to correctly solving the problem.

Hint 1 Study the clues. Find the clue that gives a specific departure time. *(Ruby Reynolds left at 7:50 P.M.)*

Hint 2 Find the other clue that mentions Ruby Reynolds. Use this clue to determine another departure time. *(Opal Owen left 2 hours and 50 minutes after Ruby. Opal left at 10:40 P.M.)*

Hint 3 Continue working through the remaining clues in this manner until you identify the thief.

Answer Key Peter Platinum stole the Destiny Diamond.

Guest	Departure Time
Sam Silver	9:15 P.M.
Susie Sapphire	8:35 P.M.
Jeffrey Jade	10:10 P.M.
Ruby Reynolds	7:50 P.M.
Diamond Diaz	9:30 P.M.
Peter Platinum	8:05 P.M.
Patty Pearl	9:45 P.M.
Opal Owen	10:40 P.M.
Garth Gold	9:50 P.M.
Amelia Amethyst	10:05 P.M.

Bonus Box answer: 2 hours, 50 minutes (7:50 P.M. to 10:40 P.M.)

Time for a Mystery

POW! #21

Marcia the museum guide led ten famous jewel collectors through the Museum of Fine Jewels. After touring each exhibit, the group gathered in the dining hall for refreshments.

Later that night, the guests left one at a time. As she was turning off the lights, Marcia discovered that the Destiny Diamond was missing!

Suddenly a team of police officers burst into the museum. Officer Justus explained, "The silent jewel detector went off at 8:05 P.M. Sorry we're late, but there was a huge traffic jam on Main Street."

"The detector must have gone off when the thief left the museum," said Marcia. She checked the security guard's log, which gave the time that each guest left.

How would Marcia ever figure out who snatched the diamond?

- Sam Silver left 1 hour and 25 minutes before Opal Owen.
- Susie Sapphire left 90 minutes before Amelia Amethyst.
- Jeffrey Jade left 55 minutes after Sam Silver.
- Ruby Reynolds left at 7:50 P.M.
- Diamond Diaz left 15 minutes before Patty Pearl.
- Peter Platinum left 105 minutes before Garth Gold.
- Patty Pearl left 25 minutes before Jeffrey Jade.
- Opal Owen left 2 hours and 50 minutes after Ruby Reynolds.
- Garth Gold left 75 minutes after Susie Sapphire.
- Amelia Amethyst left 35 minutes after Diamond Diaz.

Now It's Your Turn
Figure out when each guest left. Then identify which jewel collector stole the Destiny Diamond!

Bonus Box: How much time passed between the first and last guests' departure times?

Sweet Solutions

Using logical reasoning to find a quantity of fudge

Problem-solving strategies
students could use:
- use logical reasoning
- make a table
- draw a picture
- work backward

Math skills
students will use:
- write number sentences correctly
- organize information

Restating the problem: Frankie lost track of the amount of fudge made at his factory. He sold his fudge in one-inch squares. Use the story clues and the pan size chart to figure out how much fudge was made.

Important information found in the problem:
- Three jumbo pans were used.
- Three times as many medium pans as jumbo pans were used.
- There were two fewer large pans than medium pans.
- Nine more extra small pans were used compared to the large pans.
- The number of small pans used was one-fourth the number of extra small pans.
- Fudge was sold in one-inch squares.

Answer Key Frankie's factory made 871 pieces of fudge.

pan size	number of pans	number of fudge pieces per pan	total number of fudge pieces
jumbo	3	8 x 10 = 80	80 x 3 = 240
large	7	6 x 7 = 42	42 x 7 = 294
medium	9	5 x 5 = 25	25 x 9 = 225
small	4	3 x 4 = 12	12 x 4 = 48
extra small	16	2 x 2 = 4	4 x 16 = 64

240 + 294 + 225 + 48 + 64 = 871

Bonus Box answer: Frankie will make $217.75 (871 x $0.25 = $217.75).

Helpful Hints
Share this information when students get stuck to help put them back on the path to correctly solving the problem.

Hint 1 How many of each pan were used? Use logic to figure this out.

Hint 2 How many pieces of fudge does each pan size hold? *(Multiply the dimensions of each pan to find its area, because each pan is measured in inches and each fudge piece is a one-inch square.)*

Hint 3 How many total fudge pieces were made with each pan size? *(Multiply the number of pans by the number of pieces in each pan.)*

Hint 4 Think about how to find the total number of fudge pieces.

POW! #22

Sweet Solutions

Business is booming at Frankie's Fudge Factory!

Frankie likes to keep track of how much fudge is made each day. Unfortunately, Frankie was so busy today that he wasn't able to keep track of the fudge amounts.

Luckily, Frankie caught his assistant, Frannie, just as she was getting ready to put the cleaned fudge pans away.

Frankie noticed that 3 jumbo pans were used. He saw that 3 times as many medium pans as jumbo pans were washed. There were 2 fewer large pans than medium pans. Nine more extra small pans were used compared to the large pans. He also saw that the number of small pans used was $\frac{1}{4}$ the number of extra small pans.

Frankie was so relieved! Since he sold his fudge in 1-inch squares, he could look at the pan size chart to help him figure out how much fudge was made. Frannie saved the day!

Fudge Pan Sizes

Jumbo—8" x 10"
Large—6" x 7"
Medium—5" x 5"
Small—3" x 4"
Extra Small—2" x 2"

Now It's Your Turn

Help Frankie figure out how much fudge he made at his factory. Use the pan size chart and the clues in the story to help you.

Bonus Box: If Frankie sells each piece of fudge for $0.25, how much will he make if he sells every piece?

Just for Kicks

Listing all the possible uniform combinations

Problem-solving strategies
students could use:
- make an organized list
- find a pattern
- draw a picture

Math skills
students will use:
- determine possible combinations
- identify probability

Restating the problem: The three captains of the Dynamite soccer team were having trouble deciding on a uniform combination. There were three pieces to the uniform—a jersey, shorts, and a headband—and three colors to choose from—red, blue, and gold. What were all the possible combinations that could have been made with these choices? Which girl was most likely to get her choice?

Important information found in the problem:
- There were three pieces to the uniform—a jersey, shorts, and a headband.
- Each piece came in three colors—red, blue, and gold.
- Katie wanted to wear two red pieces.
- Kerry wanted to wear blue shorts and a blue jersey.
- Kathy wanted to wear at least one gold piece.

Answer Key
There were 27 possible combinations.
Kathy was most likely to get her choice because there were 19 combinations with at least one gold piece.
R—red, B—blue, G—gold
J—jersey, S—shorts, H—headband

RJ, RS, RH	BJ, BS, BH	GJ, GS, GH	RJ, BS, GH
RJ, RS, BH	BJ, BS, RH	GJ, GS, RH	RJ, GS, BH
RJ, RS, GH	BJ, BS, GH	GJ, GS, BH	BJ, RS, GH
RJ, BS, RH	BJ, RS, BH	GJ, RS, GH	BJ, GS, RH
RJ, GS, RH	BJ, GS, BH	GJ, BS, GH	GJ, RS, BH
BJ, RS, RH	RJ, BS, BH	RJ, GS, GH	GJ, BS, RH
GJ, RS, RH	GJ, BS, BH	BJ, GS, GH	

Helpful Hints
Share this information when students get stuck to help put them back on the path to correctly solving the problem.

Hint 1 Make an organized list. Begin with combinations in which all pieces are the same color.

Hint 2 Now show all the combinations with two pieces of the same color. Try red first. What would be one example? *(red jersey, red shorts, blue headband)*

Hint 3 Find the combinations with two blue pieces. Then find the combinations with two gold pieces.

Hint 4 Now think of all the combinations in which each piece is a different color.

Bonus Box answer: There would be nine possible combinations.

RJ, RS	BJ, BS	GJ, GS
RJ, BS	BJ, RS	GJ, RS
RJ, GS	BJ, GS	GJ, BS

Name(s) _____ Problem solving

Just for Kicks

The captains of the Dynamite soccer team were meeting to choose a uniform combination for Saturday's game. Katie, Kathy, and Kerry couldn't seem to agree on a combination.

The Dynamite uniform had a jersey, shorts, and a headband. Each piece came in three colors— red, blue, and gold. Katie wanted to wear two red pieces. Kerry would have been happy if they each wore a blue jersey and blue shorts. Kathy just wanted to be able to wear at least one gold piece.

When their coach stepped onto the field, he overheard the girls' conversation and offered to help. The coach suggested that the girls write all the different combinations on slips of paper and put them in a cap. Then he would have one of them draw a slip to choose the combination the team would wear for the game. The girls liked the idea and immediately started to work.

Not long after they began, all the combinations were listed and placed in the cap. The coach asked Katie to reach into the cap and pull out the winning combination.

Now It's Your Turn
How many possible combinations did Katie have to pick from? Which girl was most likely to get her choice? Why?

Bonus Box: If the coach left the headband out of the uniform, how many possible combinations would there be?

©The Education Center, Inc. • *POW! Problem of the Week* • TEC915   77

Snowed Over!

Using clues to figure out three-digit numbers

Problem-solving strategies
students could use:
- guess and check
- logical reasoning

Math skills
students will use:
- number sense
- compute basic facts
- identify place values
- understand multiples, products, divisibility, and palindromes

Restating the problem: Use the clues to figure out each three-digit locker combination.

Important information found in the problem:
- Each locker combination is a three-digit number.
- The club president used clues to figure out each combination.

Answer Key
Ice—565
Skeet—120
Slick—670
Avalanche—765
Chilly—462
Flake—248

Bonus Box answer: Numbers and clues will vary.

Helpful Hints
Share this information when students get stuck to help put them back on the path to correctly solving the problem.

Hint 1 A number palindrome is a number that can be written the same way backward and forward, such as 636 and 515.

Hint 2 Consecutive digits are digits that are in order from least to greatest, such as 345, or greatest to least, such as 876.

Hint 3 To find the sum of the digits for a given number, add the digits. For example, the sum of the digits in 524 is 11 (5 + 2 + 4 = 11).

Hint 4 The multiple of a digit can be found by multiplying that digit by any whole number. For example, 32 is a multiple of 8 because 8 x 4 = 32.

Hint 5 The product of two digits is found by multiplying the digits.

Snowed Over!

Members of the Snowyvale Snowboarding Club keep their boards and other equipment in computer-controlled lockers.

Today is the big snowboarding competition. To everyone's surprise, the computer went haywire and mixed up all the 3-digit combinations used to open the lockers!

The club president found the clues he listed for each snowboarder's locker combination. Now he must work through the clues to figure out the 6 numbers and reenter them into the computer.

Can he do it in time for the big competition?

Ice's Secret Code
- palindrome
- divisible by 5
- sum of the digits is divisible by 8

Skeet's Secret Code
- multiple of 10
- largest digit is in the tens place
- sum of the digits is 3

Slick's Secret Code
- divisible by 10
- digit in the tens place is 1 greater than the digit in the hundreds place
- sum of the digits is 13

Avalanche's Secret Code
- odd
- divisible by 9
- digits in consecutive order
- digit in hundreds place is greater than the digit in the ones place

Chilly's Secret Code
- even
- digit in the tens place is divisible by 2 and 3
- sum of the digits in the ones and hundreds places is equal to the digit in the tens place
- digit in the ones place is less than the digit in the hundreds place
- no repeating digits

Flake's Secret Code
- even
- divisible by 4
- product of the tens and hundreds digits is equal to the digit in the ones place
- tens digit is 4
- no repeating digits

Now It's Your Turn
Use the clues to figure out each 3-digit number.

Bonus Box: Create two 3-digit secret codes. List a set of clues for each number. Exchange clues with a classmate and solve.

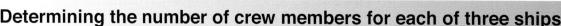

POW! #25

Determining the number of crew members for each of three ships

Teacher Page

Problem-solving strategies

students could use:
- choose an operation
- guess and check

Math skills

students will use:
- interpret one-half, twice, and five times as many
- solve for missing terms
- add
- divide

Restating the problem: Explorer I. C. Landahead put out a call for hardworking sailors to fill his ships. How many people arrived during each hour? How many people arrived all together? How many people did I. C. send home? How many people did he send to each ship?

Important information found in the problem:
- During the first hour, 23 people arrived. Five times as many people arrived the second hour. The same number of people arrived the third hour as the first and second hours combined.
- I. C. hired every third person.
- I. C. filled the *Santa Claude* with half the crew members.
- The *Pinto* had six more crew members than the *Niño*.

Answer Key *Santa Claude*—46 people, *Pinto*—26 people, *Niño*—20 people
In the first hour, 23 people arrived.
In the second hour, 115 people arrived (23 x 5 = 115).
In the third hour, 138 people arrived (23 + 115 = 138).
In all, 276 people arrived (23 + 115 + 138 = 276).
I. C. hired 92 people (276 ÷ 3 = 92).
The *Santa Claude* had 46 people (92 ÷ 2 = 46), the *Pinto* had 26 people, and the *Niño* had 20 people (26 is 6 more than 20).

Bonus Box answer: The king and queen hired 46 people and turned down 138 people (276 − 92 = 184; 184 ÷ 4 = 46; 184 − 46 = 138).

Helpful Hints
Share this information when students get stuck to help put them back on the path to correctly solving the problem.

Hint 1 Think about how many people arrived the second hour. Which operation can you use to figure this out? *(multiplication—23 x 5 = 115)* Which operation can you use to figure out how many people arrived the third hour? *(addition—23 + 115 = 138)*

Hint 2 Which operation can you use to figure out how many people were hired? *(division— 276 ÷ 3 = 92)*

Hint 3 Which operation can you use to figure out how many people were sent to the *Santa Claude*? *(division—92 ÷ 2 = 46)*

Hint 4 Think about the number of people who were sent to the *Pinto* and the *Niño*. Choose two numbers that you think might work. How can you tell if your guesses are correct? *(Verify that the sum of the two numbers is 46 and their difference is 6.)*

Name(s) _____

Sailing the High Seas

The world-famous explorer I. C. Landahead was setting out in search of new land. The king and queen of his home country gave him three ships—the *Niño,* the *Pinto,* and the *Santa Claude.* Before I. C. set out to discover new land, he hired his crew members.

I. C. first put up posters all over town calling for hardworking sailors. He was disappointed when only 23 people arrived the first hour. Then 5 times as many sailors arrived the second hour! The same number of people arrived the third hour as the first and second hours combined. After he interviewed all of the people, he decided to hire every third person and send the others home.

After I. C. selected his crew members, he filled up his ships. The *Santa Claude* was twice as large as each of the other two ships, so he filled it with half the crew members he hired. Then he divided the remaining people so that the *Pinto* had six more crew members than the *Niño.*

With his crew on board, I. C. was ready to hit the high seas!

Now It's Your Turn
Figure out how many crew members I. C. put on each ship.

Bonus Box: The king and queen interviewed the people whom I. C. did not hire. They hired $\frac{1}{4}$ of the people to work in their palace. How many workers did they hire? How many workers did they turn down?

Wild and Wacky Weeds

Using a pattern to determine the number of weeds in a garden

Problem-solving strategies
students could use:
- find a pattern
- make a table
- write an equation

Math skills
students will use:
- multiply
- add

Restating the problem: A fast-spreading weed invaded Greg's garden. If a single weed sprouted two more weeds each night, how many weeds would have been in the garden on the seventh day?

Important information found in the problem:
- The first weed appeared in Greg's garden on Sunday morning.
- For each existing weed, two more sprouted overnight.
- If there was one weed the first day, there would have been three weeds the second day, nine weeds the third day, and so on.
- Greg needed to figure out how many weeds would have invaded his garden by Saturday morning.

(Answer Key) There would have been 729 weeds by Saturday morning.

Day	Number of Weeds	Number of Weeds That Grow Overnight	Total
1	1	2	3
2	3	6	9
3	9	18	27
4	27	54	81
5	81	162	243
6	243	486	729
7	729		

Bonus Box answer: It would have taken 5 days. The Exterminator destroyed 50 weeds the first day, 100 weeds the second day, 200 weeds the third day, 400 weeds the fourth day, and 800 weeds the fifth day (50 + 100 + 200 + 400 + 800 = 1,550).

Helpful Hints
Share this information when students get stuck to help put them back on the path to correctly solving the problem.

Hint 1 How did the Multiplying Monster grow? *(Each weed sprouted 2 more weeds overnight.)*

Hint 2 Make a table to keep track of the number of weeds. What should be the headings? *(See the table in the key.)*

Hint 3 Record the number of weeds that appeared on Sunday (Day 1) in the table *(1)*. How many weeds sprouted overnight? *(2)* How many weeds were there in all? *(3)* Explain your answer. *(A weed sprouted 2 more overnight. That made 3 weeds all together.)*

Hint 4 For the second day, remember to record the total number of weeds from the first day. Then follow the pattern to find the total number of weeds for each day.

Wild and Wacky Weeds

Greg the gardener had a thorn of a problem. On Sunday morning he discovered a frightening new weed called the Multiplying Monster.

He rushed inside to get his gardening book and flipped to the section about weeds. His eyes grew wide with fear as he read about what this monster of a weed would do.

Greg discovered that for each existing weed, 2 more sprouted overnight. If there was 1 weed the first day, there would be 3 weeds the second day, 9 weeds the third day, and so on. They would continue to multiply until the garden was sprayed with a weed killer powerful enough to destroy every single weed.

Greg whipped out a calculator to figure out how many weeds would invade his garden by the following Saturday morning. Then he called every store in town to find a weed killer. He had to work fast before the wild weeds choked his precious plants!

Now It's Your Turn

How many Multiplying Monster weeds would have invaded Greg's garden by Saturday morning? Remember that for each weed, 2 new ones grew overnight.

Bonus Box: A new weed spray called The Exterminator destroys 50 weeds the first day, 100 the second day, 200 the third day, and so on. If it continued to double in power every day, how many days would it have taken to destroy 1,000 weeds?

Elevator Escapades

Drawing a picture to find the number of floors Annie passes on an elevator

Teacher Page

Problem-solving strategies
students could use:
- draw a picture
- make an organized list
- look for patterns

Math skills
students will use:
- order and sequence numbers
- add
- identify patterns

Restating the problem: Annie lives on the 11th floor of a 21-story apartment building. When she gets on the elevator, she rides all the way to the top. Then she rides down to the second floor, up to the 20th floor, and then down to the third floor. How many floors will she have passed when she finally stops at the 11th floor?

Important information found in the problem:
- There are 21 floors in Annie's apartment building.
- Annie gets on the elevator at the first floor.
- She rides all the way to the 21st floor the first time. She then rides down to the second floor. Annie then rides up to the 20th floor and then down to the third floor. Annie continues riding up and down in this manner until she reaches her floor.
- Annie lives on the 11th floor.

Answer Key Written explanations may vary. Annie passes 190 floors before ending her trip on the 11th floor. (When she begins on the 1st floor, she passes 19 floors to get to floor 21. Since she begins on the first floor, the first floor she passes is the 2nd floor. She ends on floor 21, so it doesn't count as being passed either.)

Bonus Box answer: Annie passes 135 more floors in her dad's office building. She passes 325 floors in the office building. 325 − 190 = 135.

Helpful Hints

Share this information when students get stuck to help put them back on the path to correctly solving the problem.

Hint 1 Look at where Annie begins and ends her first elevator ride. What does it mean to *pass* a floor? *(She goes by the floor but does not stop there.)* Try drawing a picture.

Hint 2 On the first ride, does Annie pass the first floor? *(No, because that is where she begins. She is already on that floor.)* Does Annie pass the 21st floor? *(No, she stops there. The elevator does not go by that floor.)*

Hint 3 Which floors are passed as Annie travels from the first floor to the 21st floor? *(2nd–20th)* How many floors are between the first and 21st floors? *(19)*

Hint 4 When Annie rides back down to the second floor, what do you notice about the number of floors passed this time? *(There are 18 floors passed, 1 less than the first ride.)*

Hint 5 What can you do to figure out the total number of floors passed? *(Add them all.)*

Elevator Escapades

Annie's life is full of ups and downs. It has to be. She is a world-famous yo-yo champion. Annie loves to yo-yo so much that she has even found a way to yo-yo ride the elevator in her apartment building.

Annie lives on the 11th floor of a 21-story apartment building. Every day when she gets on the elevator at the 1st floor, she rides all the way to the top. Next, Annie presses the button for the 2nd floor and rides down. She then takes the elevator up to the 20th floor, then down to the 3rd, then up to the 19th, and so on until she reaches her floor. By the time Annie gets off the elevator, she has passed many floors and annoyed a lot of neighbors!

One day, as Annie finally stepped off the elevator, a woman on her way to work said, "I hope I'm not late for my meeting. Do you have any idea how many floors you just passed?"

"I'm sorry," said Annie, "I've never thought about it. But I'll find out."

Annie returned to her apartment and worked on the answer to the woman's question. When she was finished, she was very happy she didn't yo-yo walk the stairs!

Now It's Your Turn
Find out how many floors Annie passes each time she yo-yo rides the elevator.

Bonus Box: Annie also likes to yo-yo ride the elevator when she visits her dad's 27-floor office building. He works on the 14th floor. How many more floors does she pass at the office building than at home?

Snow Flake and the Seven Elves

Using logic to solve a riddle

Teacher Page

Problem-solving strategies

students could use:
- logical reasoning
- write an equation
- guess and check

Math skills

students will use:
- add and subtract whole numbers
- multiply by 12
- double amounts

Restating the problem: Snow Flake must bake cookies by the dozen so that there are the fewest possible leftovers. How many cookies should she bake for each friend and for herself? How many cookies should she bake all together?

Important information found in the problem:
- Elvis gets half a dozen cookies.
- Eli gets two cookies. Elliot gets twice as many cookies as Eli.
- Snow Flake gets five more cookies than Elliot.
- Edgar and Evan get ten cookies in all. Edgar gets four more cookies than Evan.
- Eggbert and Ed get the same number of cookies.
- Snow Flake must bake the lowest number of cookies necessary—by the dozen.
- There should be the fewest possible cookies left over.

Answer Key Snow Flake should bake 36 cookies in all (3 dozen).
Elvis—6, Eli—2, Elliot—4, Snow Flake—9, Edgar—7, Evan—3, Eggbert—2, Ed—2. There will be 1 cookie left over.

Bonus Box answer: One possible solution:
Box 1: Snow Flake (9 cookies)
Box 2: Elvis and Evan (6 + 3 = 9 cookies)
Box 3: Eli and Edgar (2 + 7 = 9 cookies)
Box 4: Elliot, Eggbert, and Ed (4 + 2 + 2 + 1 extra = 9 cookies)

Helpful Hints

Share this information when students get stuck to help put them back on the path to correctly solving the problem.

Hint 1 How many cookies does Elvis get? *(6 cookies)*

Hint 2 How many cookies does Eli get? *(2 cookies)* Elliot? *(2 + 2 = 4 cookies)* Snow Flake? *(4 + 5 = 9 cookies)*

Hint 3 How many cookies do Edgar and Evan get all together? *(10 cookies)* How many does each elf get? *(Edgar—7 cookies, Evan—3 cookies)*

Hint 4 How many cookies are there so far? *(31 cookies)* How many dozens of cookies should Snow Flake bake to account for this number? *(3 dozen)*

Hint 5 If Snow Flake bakes this number and there should be the fewest possible extra cookies, how many cookies should Eggbert and Ed each receive? *(2 cookies each)*

Name(s)_____ Problem solving

Snow Flake and the Seven Elves

Snow Flake decided to bake cookies to share with her seven best friends: Elvis, Eli, Elliot, Edgar, Evan, Eggbert, and Ed. She sent a note to find out how many cookies she should bake. The elves sent their reply in the form of a rhyming riddle:

Thanks for your cookie offer.
Oh, how we love them so!
To bake the correct number,
Here's what you need to know:

Elvis eats half a dozen.
Eli's pleased with just 2.
Double Eli's number for Elliot.
Bake 5 more than that for *you.*

Bake 4 more for Edgar than Evan.
(They'll have a total of 10.)
Make an equal number for Eggbert
   and Ed,
And be sure to bake by the dozen!

Snow Flake smiled at their clever response. She decided to bake the lowest number of cookies necessary to feed everyone. Then she would pass them out so that there were the fewest possible cookies left over.

Now It's Your Turn
How many cookies will Snow Flake and each friend receive? How many cookies should she bake in all? Remember that she must bake the cookies by the dozen.

Bonus Box: Snow Flake decided to package the cookies in 4 boxes, each containing the same number. Draw the 4 boxes and label each one with its owners' names. Be sure to put any leftover cookies in a box.

©The Education Center, Inc. • POW! Problem of the Week • TEC915   87

Chalk Dust

Determining how long a box of chalk will last

Problem-solving strategies

students could use:

- draw a picture
- look for patterns
- guess and check

Math skills

students will use:

- use patterns
- add or multiply fractions

Restating the problem: Miss Richards uses ³/₄ of a piece of chalk each day. She sets aside each leftover quarter. On the fifth day, she joins the four quarter pieces of chalk to make one whole piece. How many days will her 16-piece box of chalk last?

Important information found in the problem:

- The box of chalk contains 16 pieces.
- Miss Richards uses ³/₄ of a piece of chalk each day.
- Every fifth day, she combines the four leftover quarter pieces to make one whole piece.

(**Answer Key**) Miss Richards's box will last 21 days. She will have ¹/₄ of a piece left over. Written explanations may vary. If ³/₄ of a piece of chalk is used each day for 16 days, 16 quarters remain. Miss Richards combines the 16 quarter pieces to make 4 whole pieces (¹/₄ x 16 = 4). Those pieces will last 4 days with 4 quarters left over. Miss Richards then combines those 4 quarters to make 1 more whole piece (¹/₄ x 4 = 1). That whole piece will last her 1 day with ¹/₄ of a piece remaining (16 + 4 + 1 = 21).

Bonus Box answer: Miss Richards will need to order nine boxes. One box of chalk will last 21 days with ¹/₄ of a piece left over. Eight boxes will last 170 days. (21 x 8 = 168; ¹/₄ x 8 = 2; 168 + 2 = 170) Since there are 180 days in the school year, she'll need to order one more box to have enough.

Helpful Hints

Share this information when students get stuck to help put them back on the path to correctly solving the problem.

Hint 1 How many days will one piece of chalk last? *(1)* How much will Miss Richards have left over? *(¹/₄ of a piece)*

Hint 2 Think about the leftover chalk. How many pieces will be left over after 16 days? *(16 quarter pieces)*

Hint 3 Think about the number of whole pieces that can be made with the leftover chalk. How can you figure that out? *(Add 1 quarter 16 times. That equals 4 whole pieces.)*

Hint 4 Think about the number of days she can use the new pieces. Will she have any left over? *(She can use that chalk for 4 days. She'll have 4 quarters left over.)*

Hint 5 With the remaining chalk, can she get another whole piece? *(Yes, because 4 quarters equal 1 whole.)*

Hint 6 Remember her policy. Will Miss Richards have anything left over after she uses the last whole piece? *(Yes, she'll have ¹/₄ of a piece.)*

POW! #29

Chalk Dust

Sara's teacher, Miss Richards, never likes to waste anything.

When the kids make crafts, Miss Richards collects all the scraps of construction paper to use again. Any leftover food scraps from the kids' snacks are thrown outside for the birds. She brings in her old T-shirts to use as smocks in the classroom. Miss Richards even hates to waste chalk!

One day, Sara gave Miss Richards a brand-new 16-piece box of chalk. The students in Miss Richards's class noticed that she used only $\frac{3}{4}$ of a piece of chalk that day. Then she took out a new piece of chalk the next day.

Sara asked Miss Richards why she wasn't using the last $\frac{1}{4}$ of the piece. Miss Richards replied that the remaining piece of chalk was too small for her to hold. However, she did not throw it away. She just set it aside.

On the fifth morning, Miss Richards did not take out a new piece of chalk. The kids watched as she joined the 4 quarter pieces to make 1 whole piece. "Interesting," thought Sara. "I guess that's one way to stretch a box of chalk!"

Now It's Your Turn
Help Sara figure out how many days Miss Richards's box of chalk will last.

Bonus Box: Miss Richards wants to make sure she has enough chalk for the entire 180-day school year. How many boxes of chalk will she need?

Robin's Roman Numerals

Making an organized list of roman numerals

Teacher Page

Problem-solving strategies

students could use:

- make an organized list
- find a pattern
- act it out
- use logical reasoning

Math skills

students will use:

- understand roman numerals
- order and sequence numbers
- add and subtract

Restating the problem: Robin buys pins with letters to represent roman numerals. She wants to wear a different combination of pins each day for the 180 days of school. How many pins of each letter will she need to buy?

Important information found in the problem:
- Robin needs an I pin for one, a V pin for five, an X pin for ten, an L pin for 50, and a C pin for 100.
- She needs two I pins for the second day.
- She needs three I pins for the third day.
- Robin needs an I and a V for the fourth day.
- Robin will wear a different combination for each day of school.

Answer Key Robin needs at least 10 pins. She will need 3 I pins, 1 V pin, 4 X pins, 1 L pin, and 1 C pin.

Days with 1 pin: I, V, X, L, C
Days with 2 pins: II, IV, VI, IX, XI, XV, XX, XL, LI, LV, LX, XC, CI, CV, CX, CL
Days with 3 pins: III, VII, XII, XIV, XVI, XIX, XXI, XXV, XXX, XLI, XLV, LII, LIV, LVI, LIX, LXI, LXV, LXX, XCI, XCV, CII, CIV, CVI, CIX, CXI, CXV, CXX, CXL, CLI, CLV, CLX
Days with 4 pins: VIII, XIII, XVII, XXII, XXIV, XXVI, XXIX, XXXI, XXXV, XLII, XLIV, XLVI, XLIX, LIII, LVII, LXII, LXIV, LXVI, LXIX, LXXI, LXXV, LXXX, XCII, XCIV, XCVI, XCIX, CIII, CVII, CXII, CXIV, CXVI, CXIX, CXXI, CXXV, CXXX, CXLI, CXLV, CLII, CLIV, CLVI, CLIX, CLXI, CLXV, CLXX
Days with 5 pins: XVIII, XXIII, XXVII, XXXII, XXXIV, XXXVI, XXXIX, XLIII, XLVII, LVIII, LXIII LXVII, LXXII, LXXIV, LXXVI, LXXIX, LXXXI, LXXXV, XCIII, XCVII, CVIII, CXIII, CXVII, CXXII, CXXIV, CXXVI, CXXIX, CXXXI, CXXXV, CXLII, CXLIV, CXLVI, CXLIX, CLIII, CLVII, CLXII, CLXIV, CLXVI, CLXIX, CLXXI, CLXXV, CLXXX
Days with 6 pins: XXVIII, XXXIII, XXXVII, XLVIII, LXVIII, LXXIII, LXXVII, LXXXII, LXXXIV, LXXXVI, LXXXIX, XCVIII, CXVIII, CXXIII, CXXVII, CXXXII, CXXXIV, CXXXVI, CXXXIX, CXLIII, CXLVII, CLVIII, CLXIII, CLXVII, CLXXII, CLXXIV, CLXXVI, CLXXIX
Days with 7 pins: XXXVIII, LXXVIII, LXXXIII, LXXXVII, CXXVIII, CXXXIII, CXXXVII, CXLVIII, CLXVIII, CLXXIII, CLXXVII
Days with 8 pins: LXXXVIII, CXXXVIII, CLXXVIII

Helpful Hints

Share this information when students get stuck to help put them back on the path to correctly solving the problem.

Hint 1 Write the numbers 1–100. Beside each number, write its matching roman numeral.

Hint 2 Remember to add the roman numerals to determine how many there are. For example, if you have III, each I equals one: 1 + 1 + 1 = 3.

Hint 3 What happens when you get to the roman numeral for four? *(The I goes to the left of the V, and you have to subtract.)* What about the number nine? *(The I goes to the left of the X.)* Think about that each time you come to a number with a four or a nine in it.

Hint 4 The greater value always comes first in a roman numeral unless the number includes a four or nine (14, 19, 24, 29, etc.).

Hint 5 What shortcut can you use to write the roman numerals for 101–180? *(Repeat the roman numerals for 1–80. Include a C in front of each one.)*

Bonus Box answer: The most pins Robin will wear is 8. She will wear them on the 88th day (LXXXVIII), the 138th day (CXXXVIII), and the 178th day (CLXXVIII) of school.

Robin's Roman Numerals

POW! #30

Robin was having a fantastic time on her vacation. After all, she was in Rome!

She loved everything about the city—the people, the food, and the sights. Before heading home, Robin decided she wanted a souvenir. She searched high and low looking for the perfect one, but nothing seemed quite right.

Robin made one last stop in a jewelry store. She was about to give up on her search when her mom pointed out some pins with letters hanging on a wall.

Days I'll need one pin—I, V,...
Days I'll need two pins—II, IV, VI,...
Days I'll need three pins—III, VII,...
Days I'll need four pins—VIII,...

"How about some roman numerals to help you remember Rome?" her mother suggested. "You can wear a different set of pins for each of the 180 days of school."

Robin thought for a moment, smiled, and exclaimed, "Perfect!" Looking at the pins she said, "I'll need an I for one, a V for five, an X for ten, an L for 50, and a C for 100. I'll need two Is for the second day, three Is for the third day, and four Is for—no, an I and a V for the fourth day."

Robin grabbed a pencil and some paper from her bag and began to work. A short time later she was at the counter purchasing her souvenir pins.

Now It's Your Turn
What is the least number of pins Robin needs to buy? How many of each letter will she need to be able to make each roman numeral from 1 to 180?

Bonus Box: What are the most pins Robin will wear at any one time? On what days will she wear them?

Monster Motel

Finding prime numbers given a set of clues

Teacher Page

Problem-solving strategies
students could use:
- guess and check
- logical reasoning

Math skills
students will use:
- name prime numbers
- divide numbers
- identify place value

Restating the problem: Which five rooms out of 60 are available if the room numbers are prime and have the same digit in the ones place?

Important information found in the problem:
- There are 60 rooms, numbered 1 to 60.
- There are five empty rooms.
- All the empty room numbers are prime.
- The empty rooms all have the same digit in the ones place.

Answer Key The empty rooms are numbers 3, 13, 23, 43, and 53.

Bonus Box answer: Scary—3, Gary—13, Harry—23, Larry—43, Barry—53

Helpful Hints

Share this information when students get stuck to help put them back on the path to correctly solving the problem.

Hint 1 The empty room numbers are prime. What does this mean? *(Each number is only divisible by 1 and itself.)*

Hint 2 List the prime numbers up to 60 *(2, 3, 5, 7, 11, 13, 17, 19, 23, 29, 31, 37, 41, 43, 47, 53, 59).*

Hint 3 What is the first prime number? *(2)* Can this be one of the empty rooms? *(No, because the other numbers in the series that have a 2 in the ones place—12, 22, 32, etc.—are not prime.)*

Monster Motel

After a rough night of howling and prowling, Harry and his four beastly brothers were tired. They decided to rest their heads at a motel.

The motel's night clerk didn't look very happy to see the fearsome family. They appeared harmless enough, even a little cute. But he didn't like monsters, and these didn't look too smart. Maybe he could trick them into finding a different motel!

"This motel has 60 rooms numbered 1 to 60," the clerk told Harry. "If you can figure out which 5 rooms are available, you can stay here for the night. All the 5 room numbers are prime numbers. Also, the room numbers all have the same digit in the ones place." The clerk smirked, sure that he was rid of the creatures for the night.

Harry explained the situation to his four brothers, and they put their seven heads together. They were a lot smarter than the night clerk thought, but this would take some time.

Now It's Your Turn
Help Harry and his brothers figure out which 5 motel rooms are empty.

Bonus Box: After getting the room keys, each monster discovered that his room number matched his number of spots. Larry has 10 fewer spots than Barry. Scary has the least number of spots. Gary has fewer spots than Larry or Harry. How many spots does each brother have?

All Wrapped Up!

Working backward to find out how many rolls of wrapping paper Tom sold

POW! #32

Teacher Page

Problem-solving strategies
students could use:
- work backward
- look for patterns
- choose the correct operation
- make an organized table or chart

Math skills
students will use:
- make a list
- add
- multiply

Restating the problem: Tom sold the most wrapping-paper rolls during his school's fundraiser. How many rolls of wrapping paper did Tom sell? If he had four rolls left over, how many did he have at the beginning of the sale?

Important information found in the problem:
- Tom sold five rolls to Mr. Green.
- He sold twice as many rolls to Mrs. Red as he did to Mr. Green, plus one more.
- He sold twice as many rolls to Mrs. Blue as he did to Mrs. Red, plus two more.
- He sold twice as many rolls to Mr. Gray as he did to Mrs. Blue, plus three more.
- Tom had four rolls left over.

Answer Key Tom sold a total of 91 rolls of wrapping paper, so he received a check for $91. He could have won $95.
Mr. Green bought 5 rolls.
Mrs. Red bought 11 rolls (5 x 2 + 1 = 11).
Mrs. Blue bought 24 rolls (11 x 2 + 2 = 24).
Mr. Gray bought 51 rolls (24 x 2 + 3 = 51).
5 + 11 + 24 + 51 = 91 rolls.
91 rolls + 4 rolls left over = 95 rolls to begin with

Bonus Box answer: Tom sold 323 rolls of paper all together on Friday and Saturday.
On Friday, Tom sold twice as many rolls as he did on Thursday, plus 4 (51 x 2 + 4 = 106).
On Saturday, he sold twice as many rolls as he did on Friday, plus 5 (106 x 2 + 5 = 217).
106 + 217 = 323 rolls

Helpful Hints
Share this information when students get stuck to help put them back on the path to correctly solving the problem.

Hint 1 Look at the third paragraph again. In what order is the information given? *(in reverse)*

Hint 2 What information should come first to help guide you through the rest of the problem? *(On Monday, Tom sold five rolls to Mr. Green.)*

Hint 3 What information do you need next? *(the number he sold to Mrs. Red)* What do the words "twice as many" mean? *(multiply by 2)* How would you write the equation to figure out how many rolls Mrs. Red bought? *(5 x 2 + 1 = 11)*

Hint 4 Continue reading the problem in reverse order to figure out how many rolls each person bought.

Hint 5 How do you figure out the total number of rolls? *(Add all of the days' totals.)*

Hint 6 What do you need to do to calculate the total number of rolls Tom started with? *(Look back to see that he had four rolls left over. Then add 91 + 4 to equal 95.)*

All Wrapped Up!

Tom is a great salesman. He won the grand prize for selling the most wrapping-paper rolls for his school's fundraiser!

On Monday, each student was given the same number of wrapping-paper rolls to sell by Friday. Everyone was so surprised when Tom returned to school Friday with only 4 rolls left over. His friends asked how he was able to sell so much. Tom told them it was easy because everyone at his mom's office liked wrapping paper.

Tom then explained who bought all of his rolls. On Thursday, Mr. Gray bought twice as many rolls of wrapping paper as Mrs. Blue, plus 3 more. The day before that, Tom sold twice as many rolls to Mrs. Blue as he did to Mrs. Red, plus 2 more. On Tuesday, he sold twice as many rolls to Mrs. Red as he did to Mr. Green, plus 1 more. On Monday, he sold 5 rolls of wrapping paper to Mr. Green.

On Friday, the principal presented Tom with the grand prize—a check that equaled the number of wrapping-paper rolls he sold. When she asked him how he managed to win, Tom exclaimed, "I guess I just got all wrapped up in selling!"

Now It's Your Turn
Tom's friends want to know how much money he received. Help them figure out the amount of the check by determining how many rolls of wrapping paper Tom sold. How much could he have received if he'd sold every roll?

Bonus Box: Tom was asked to sell wrapping paper for two more days. He sold rolls on Friday afternoon and Saturday. If he sold them by continuing the pattern, how many rolls did he sell in those two days?

Butterfly Social

Guessing and checking to find out which size tables Betty Butterfly should rent

Problem-solving strategies

students could use:

- guess and check
- draw a picture
- write an equation

Math skills

students will use:

- compute mentally
- calculate perimeter

Restating the problem: Betty Butterfly needs to rent seven tables to seat 52 guests. There are three different sizes of tables. Which tables should she rent?

Important information found in the problem:

- The guests will be seated at one long row of tables that will be pushed together.
- One size of table seats two people on each side.
- Another size seats two people along the shorter sides and three people along the longer sides.
- The last size seats two people along the shorter sides and five people along the longer sides.
- Betty needs to arrange seating for exactly 52 guests.
- Betty wants to rent seven tables.

Answer Key There are two possible solutions. Betty could rent one 2 x 2 table, four 2 x 3 tables, and two 2 x 5 tables. Or she could rent three 2 x 2 tables, one 2 x 3 table, and three 2 x 5 tables. One arrangement for each solution is shown below.

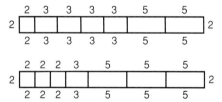

Bonus Box answer: There are 26 guests (52 ÷ 2 = 26). One table seats 14 people. The other table seats 12 people.

Helpful Hints

Share this information when students get stuck to help put them back on the path to correctly solving the problem.

Hint 1 What do the tables look like? Draw and label each one. *(Students should draw a 2 x 2 square, a 2 x 3 rectangle, and a 2 x 5 rectangle.)*

Hint 2 How many guests does one square table seat? *(8)* Now, think about the arrangement of the tables once they are pushed together. How many guests will two square tables seat after they are pushed together? *(12)* What do you notice about the number of seats available? *(Possible answer: 4 seats are lost when the tables are pushed together.)*

Hint 3 Not counting the two seats along each of the shorter ends, how many guests will each table hold? *(4, 6, and 10)*

Hint 4 Think about the final arrangement of the tables. Not counting the two seats along each of the shorter ends, how many guests will be seated at the tables? *(48)*

Hint 5 Think about how many guests each table will seat and how many guests are seated at the row of tables, not counting the two at each end. Try to write a number sentence to show the combination of seven tables.
(4 + 4 + 4 + 6 + 10 + 10 + 10 = 48 or 4 + 6 + 6 + 6 + 6 + 10 + 10 = 48)

Butterfly Social

Betty Butterfly just loves to be social!

She has invited 52 of her best friends to her annual Flutter Festival. Betty wants to seat her guests in one long row of tables that will be pushed together.

There are three sizes of tables at the party rental store. One size seats 2 people on each side. Another size seats 2 guests along the shorter sides and 3 along the longer sides. The last one seats 2 guests along the shorter sides and 5 along the longer sides.

Betty wants to rent 7 tables that will seat all her guests—no more, no less. She looked over the tables carefully.

What combination of tables should she choose?

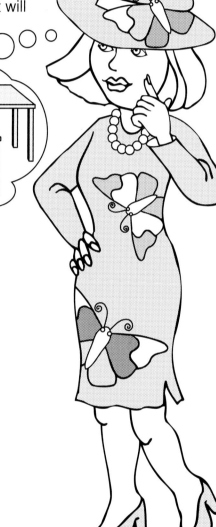

Now It's Your Turn
Help Betty Butterfly figure out which tables she should rent. Then sketch one possible table arrangement. Remember that she will push the tables together to form one long row.

Bonus Box: Betty's guest list for her next party is half as long as the one above. She wants to rent 2 tables from a different rental store. She will not push them together. One table will seat 2 more people than the other one. How many people will each table seat?

Roller Coaster Combos

Using a pattern to determine the number of roller coaster rides

Problem-solving strategies

students could use:
- make a table or chart
- find a pattern
- make an organized list

Math skills

students will use:
- write addition sentences
- add two-digit numbers

Restating the problem: What pattern did Ashley follow to invite her friends each day? Each day, how many rides did the friends take if they rode two at a time? How many times did the friends ride the roller coaster during the entire week?

Important information found in the problem:
- Only two friends could ride in the last car of the roller coaster at a time.
- Each friend rode once with each of the other friends.
- One friend joined Ashley at the park on Monday. They took one ride. Three friends joined her on Tuesday. They took six rides. Five friends joined her on Wednesday.
- Ashley's pattern of bringing more friends to the park continued on Thursday and Friday.
- Ashley rode the roller coaster with each friend.

Answer Key Ashley and her friends took 95 rides in all. An organized list may be used to find the total number of rides taken on Wednesday (see the list). Students should notice a pattern in the number sentences for finding the total number of rides (see the chart).

Wednesday—Ashley and Friends B, C, D, E, F (15 rides in all)

AB	BC	CD	DE	EF
AC	BD	CE	DF	
AD	BE	CF		
AE	BF			
AF				

Day	Friends Invited	Rides
Monday	1	1
Tuesday	3	3 + 2 + 1 = 6
Wednesday	5	5 + 4 + 3 + 2 + 1 = 15
Thursday	7	7 + 6 + 5 + 4 + 3 + 2 + 1 = 28
Friday	9	9 + 8 + 7 + 6 + 5 + 4 + 3 + 2 + 1 = 45

1 + 6 + 15 + 28 + 45 = 95 rides in all

Helpful Hints

Share this information when students get stuck to help put them back on the path to correctly solving the problem.

Hint 1 Organize the information in a chart. How many friends did Ashley invite on Monday? Tuesday? Wednesday? *(1, 3, 5)* Follow the pattern to find out how many friends she invited on Thursday and then on Friday *(7, 9)*.

Hint 2 How many friends, including Ashley, rode the roller coaster each day? *(Monday—2, Tuesday—4, Wednesday—6, Thursday—8, Friday—10)*

Hint 3 List the pairs that rode the roller coaster on Wednesday. Begin by listing the friends who rode with Ashley: Brittany, Carly, Dan, and the fifth and sixth friends, whose names you may make up. Beginning with a new column, repeat this process with Brittany, without repeating pairs. Continue with columns for the other friends. Describe the pattern that you see. *(Each column decreases by 1 pair.)* Write a number sentence for the number of pairs in the columns *(5 + 4 + 3 + 2 + 1 = 15)*.

Hint 4 Think about the relationship between the number of friends who rode the roller coaster on Wednesday and the number of rides they took. Follow this pattern to find out how many rides the friends took on Thursday and then on Friday.

Bonus Box answer: Ashley must purchase 76 tickets. She needs 95 tickets. Since every fifth ticket is free, she gets 19 free tickets (95 ÷ 5 = 19). She must pay for 76 tickets (95 − 19 = 76).

Roller Coaster Combos

Ashley is wild about roller coasters! She was first in line to ride the brand-new Brain Bender at the amusement park. She rode the roller coaster 10 times before she decided that riding in the last car was the most fun. Ashley decided to ride this car with each of her friends during the next week.

On Monday, Ashley brought her friend Zoe to the park. They took 1 roller coaster ride together.

On Tuesday, she invited 3 friends—Brittany, Carly, and Dan. Every person wanted to ride with each friend in the last car, but only 2 people could ride at a time. Before Ashley bought tickets, she figured out that she needed enough for 6 rides. First, Ashley would ride with Brittany, then with Carly, and then with Dan. Next, Brittany would ride with Carly and then with Dan. Last, Carly would ride with Dan.

On Wednesday, Ashley brought 5 friends to the park. She continued this pattern of bringing more friends to the park on Thursday and Friday. Every day, each friend wanted a chance to ride in the last car with each of the other friends. Each day, Ashley figured out how many tickets she needed for all the rides.

Now It's Your Turn
Figure out how many tickets Ashley bought each day: Wednesday, Thursday, and Friday. How many rides did Ashley and her friends take during the entire week?

Bonus Box: If Ashley gets 1 free ticket for every 4 she buys, how many tickets would she have to pay for if she buys them at the beginning of the week?

Marvelo's Math Magic

Determining two numbers that equal a given sum, product, difference, and quotient

Problem-solving strategies

students could use:
- guess and check
- logical reasoning

Math skills

students will use:
- write equations
- add
- subtract
- multiply
- divide
- number sense

Restating the problem: The Great Marvelo likes to perform magic tricks. He placed four cards with numbers into his hat: a sum (65), a difference (39), a product (676), and a quotient (4). After saying a magic word and waving his wand, he pulled out two two-digit numbers that, when added, subtracted, multiplied, and divided, result in these four answers. What are the two numbers Marvelo pulled from his hat?

Important information found in the problem:
- The sum of the two numbers is 65.
- Their difference is 39.
- Their product is 676.
- Their quotient is 4.
- The two two-digit numbers, when added, subtracted, multiplied, and divided, will equal the sum, difference, product, and quotient listed above.

Answer Key The two 2-digit numbers are 52 and 13. Written explanations will vary. 52 + 13 = 65; 52 − 13 = 39; 52 x 13 = 676; 52 ÷ 13 = 4

Bonus Box answer: 84; 42; 1,323; 3
21 + 63 = 84; 63 − 21 = 42; 63 x 21 = 1,323; 63 ÷ 21 = 3

Helpful Hints

Share this information when students get stuck to help put them back on the path to correctly solving the problem.

Hint 1 Marvelo writes the sum 65. What is a sum? *(A sum is the answer when you add 2 numbers.)* Since both numbers have two digits each, what is the smallest possible addend? *(10)* Since the sum is 65, what would be the largest possible addend? *(55)*

Hint 2 Marvelo writes the difference 39. What is a difference? *(A difference is the answer when you subtract one number from another.)* What is the difference between 55 and 10? *(45)* Can 55 and 10 be the numbers Marvelo pulls from his hat? *(No.)*

Hint 3 Since you know Marvelo did not pull 55 and 10 from his hat, try other combinations of two-digit numbers. You know the numbers must be greater than 10 and less than 55. The sum of the two numbers must equal 65.

Hint 4 Marvelo writes the quotient 4. What is a quotient? *(A quotient is the answer when you divide 2 numbers.)* What does this quotient tell you? *(One number must divide into the other number with no remainder.)*

Hint 5 Marvelo writes the product 676. What is a product? *(A product is the answer when you multiply 2 numbers.)* The two numbers should equal 676 when multiplied.

Marvelo's Math Magic

Marvin wants to be a famous magician. He calls himself "The Great Marvelo" and performs magic tricks for his friends. Marvelo performs card tricks and disappearing tricks. But his favorite tricks are math tricks. They always stump the audience!

When Marvelo begins a math trick, he quickly removes his hat. He turns it, shakes it, and taps it to show the audience that it is completely empty. Then he calls on volunteers to give him 4 numbers.

During one show, he asked for a sum and heard "65." When he asked for a difference, someone yelled, "39!" When Marvelo wanted a product, he heard "676." And when he needed a quotient, a little boy held up 4 fingers.

Marvelo wrote each number on a different card and dropped it in his hat. "Ladies and gentlemen," he announced, "I have placed all 4 numbers in my hat. I will now wave my wand, say the magic word, and pull 2 new numbers out of my hat. They will each have 2 digits. These two numbers, when added, subtracted, multiplied, and divided, will equal the sum, difference, product, and quotient that you just named."

Marvelo then pulled two numbers out of his hat, showed them to the audience, and bowed. He knew he had stumped them again!

Now It's Your Turn
What two numbers did Marvelo pull out of his hat?

Bonus Box: If Marvelo pulled out 21 and 63, what 4 numbers would he have heard from the audience?

Creepy-Crawly Café

Guessing and checking to determine what diners ordered in a restaurant

Problem-solving strategies

students could use:

- guess and check
- work backward
- make an organized table or chart

Math skills

students will use:

- estimate
- add and subtract money
- solve for missing addends
- read a menu

Restating the problem: Using the information that Gator Waiter remembers and the customers' checks, determine what each of the four diners ordered for dinner at the Creepy-Crawly Café.

Important information found in the problem:
- The price of each item is found on the menu.
- Each diner ordered something from each category on the menu.
- Spike ordered Pickled Crickets, Gigi ordered a Sand Crab Shake, and Jake and Ginger each ordered Katydid Kabobs.
- The 12 items Spike, Gigi, and Jake ordered included one of each item on the menu.
- Spike's check total was $11.11, Gigi's total was $12.22, Jake's total was $13.33, and Ginger's total was $14.44.

Answer Key

	appetizer	main dish	dessert	drink
Spike	Pickled Crickets ($3.44)	Baked Beetles ($5.62)	Honeybee Cookies ($1.60)	Bug Juice ($0.45)
Gigi	Slug Gumbo ($3.24)	Chigger Casserole ($6.20)	Caterpillar Ice Cream ($1.72)	Sand Crab Shake ($1.06)
Jake	French-Fried Ants ($2.55)	Katydid Kabobs ($7.73)	Chocolate Grasshopper ($2.21)	Moth Milk ($0.84)
Ginger	Pickled Crickets ($3.44)	Katydid Kabobs ($7.73)	Chocolate Grasshopper ($2.21)	Sand Crab Shake ($1.06)

Spike ($3.44 + $5.62 + $1.60 + $0.45 = $11.11)
Gigi ($3.24 + $ 6.20 + $1.72 + $1.06 = $12.22)
Jake ($2.55 + $7.73 + $2.21 + $0.84 = $13.33)
Ginger ($3.44 + $7.73 + $2.21 + $1.06 = $14.44)

Bonus Box answer: Both of the Bugs ordered Slug Gumbo ($3.24 each), Baked Beetles ($5.62 each), Caterpillar Ice Cream ($1.72 each), and Moth Milk ($0.84 each).

($3.24 x 2) + ($5.62 x 2) + ($1.72 x 2) + ($0.84 x 2) = $22.84

Helpful Hints

Share this information when students get stuck to help put them back on the path to correctly solving the problem.

Hint 1 Try looking at one part of the problem at a time. Start with Spike's order. What do you already know? *(Spike ordered Pickled Crickets for $3.44. His total order equaled $11.11.)*

Hint 2 Think about how much Spike had left to spend. Guess and check to figure out his remaining three items. Remember that he spent the least amount on his meal.

Hint 3 Make an organized table to help with the other orders. What do you know about Gigi's order? *(She ordered a Sand Crab Shake for $1.06 and spent $12.22. She also did not order the same things that Spike or Jake ordered.)*

Hint 4 What do you know about Jake's order? *(He ordered Katydid Kabobs and spent $13.33. He did not order the same things as Gigi or Spike.)*

Hint 5 What do you know about Ginger's order? *(She ordered Katydid Kabobs and spent $14.44.)*

Creepy-Crawly Café

POW! #36

Spike and Gigi O'Spider's favorite restaurant is the Creepy-Crawly Café. One night they met their friends Jake and Ginger LeJunebug for dinner. They were starving when they arrived! So everyone decided to order one item from each menu category.

When Gator Waiter took their first order, Spike told him that he'd start with the Pickled Crickets. Gigi was very thirsty, so she began with a Sand Crab Shake. Jake and Ginger both went straight for a main course of Katydid Kabobs.

After the friends finished the first part of their meal, Gator Waiter returned to take the rest of their order. He noted that the 12 items Spike, Gigi, and Jake ordered included one of each item on the menu.

Finally, when Gator rang up the foursome's checks, he giggled at the pattern he saw. Spike's order came to $11.11. Gigi's meal was $12.22. Jake's ticket rang up at $13.33, and Ginger's was $14.44. Unfortunately, the computer erased the actual orders!

Luckily, Gator was such a good waiter that he remembered the first courses ordered. He knew he could figure out the correct items to deliver to everyone.

Creepy-Crawly Cafe

Appetizers
French-Fried Ants.................$2.55
Pickled Crickets.....................$3.44
Slug Gumbo...........................$3.24

Main Dish
Baked Beetles........................$5.62
Chigger Casserole.................$6.20
Katydid Kabobs.....................$7.73

Dessert
Chocolate Grasshopper.........$2.21
Caterpillar Ice Cream............$1.72
Honeybee Cookies.................$1.60

Drinks
Bug Juice...............................$0.45
Moth Milk...............................$0.84
Sand Crab Shake..................$1.06

Now It's Your Turn
Help Gator figure out what Spike, Gigi, Jake, and Ginger ordered.

Bonus Box: At the table next to the foursome, the Bugs enjoyed a wonderful dinner of their own. Both of them ordered the exact same thing from each category on the menu. For starters, they enjoyed some piping hot Slug Gumbo. The couple's bill totaled $22.84. What did the Bugs have for dinner?

Captain Calculation

Finding the sum of all the numbers from 1 to 100 by discovering a pattern

Teacher Page

Problem-solving strategies
students could use:
• find a pattern
• solve a simpler problem
• make a list

Math skills
students will use:
• find sums of 100
• add one- and two-digit numbers
• multiply by 100

Restating the problem: As Captain Calculation added all the numbers from 1 to 100, he made an interesting discovery. What shortcut did he take to find the sum of all the numbers?

Important information found in the problem:
• Captain Calculation found the sum of all the numbers from 1 to 100.
• Captain Calculation looked carefully at the numbers 49 and 51.

(Answer Key) The sum of the numbers from 1 to 100 is 5,050. There are 49 pairs of addends (1 + 99, 2 + 98, 3 + 97...49 + 51) that equal 100. 49 x 100 = 4,900. The numbers 50 and 100 should be added to the sum (4,900 + 50 + 100 = 5,050).

Bonus Box answer: 1,275. There are 24 pairs of addends that equal 50. 24 x 50 = 1,200. The numbers 25 and 50 should be added to the sum (1,200 + 25 + 50 = 1,275).

Helpful Hints

Share this information when students get stuck to help put them back on the path to correctly solving the problem.

Hint 1 List the numbers 1 to 10. Pair as many numbers as possible to make sums of ten and write an equation for each one *(1 + 9, 2 + 8, 3 + 7, 4 + 6)*. How many sums of ten did you make? *(4)* What is the total of all the sums? Explain how you found your answer *(40; 4 x 10 = 40)*.

Hint 2 Which numbers were you unable to pair? *(5 and 10)* Find the sum of all ten numbers. *(40 + 5 + 10 = 55)*.

Hint 3 Look closely at the numbers 49 and 51. What do you notice about the pair? *(The sum is 100.)*

Hint 4 Think of other pairs of numbers from 1 to 100 that equal 100. List a few equations in order, beginning with 1 + 99 *(1 + 99, 2 + 98, 3 + 97...)*. What pattern do you see? *(As one addend increases by one, the other addend decreases by one.)*

Hint 5 Can you predict the last equation on the list? *(49 + 51)* Without listing them all, how many pairs of addends equal 100? *(49)* Use multiplication to find the total of all the sums *(49 x 100 = 4,900)*.

Hint 6 Which two numbers will not appear in the list? *(50 and 100)*

Captain Calculation

Faster than a calculator! Able to multiply large numbers in a single bound! Meet Captain Calculation, known worldwide for his speedy computation skills. This mathematical superhero soars through the skies in search of challenging math problems to solve.

One day, as Captain Calculation flew over an elementary school, his supersensitive ears overheard a problem that made his number-filled head spin! Ms. Dee Vide, the teacher, asked her students to find the sum of all the numbers from 1 to 100!

Still flying in circles above the school, Captain Calculation began to add the numbers in his head. The more numbers he added, the more confused he became. "There has to be a shortcut," he thought.

Captain Calculation landed on the school roof and pulled out some paper and a pencil. He wrote the numbers 1 to 51 and scratched his head. He looked carefully at the numbers 49 and 51.

Suddenly, our hero saw the solution as clearly as a bolt of lightning! He solved the problem in less than two minutes.

Captain Calculation flew into the classroom, wrote the answer on the board, and took off to solve another math challenge!

Now It's Your Turn

Captain Calculation had the correct answer but flew away before he explained how he found it! How did he find the sum of all the numbers from 1 to 100 so quickly? Help the students figure out his shortcut.

Bonus Box: Find the sums of the numbers from 1 to 50. Remember to look for a shortcut.

An All-Star Challenge

Figuring out how many baskets a player made and missed

Teacher Page

Problem-solving strategies

students could use:

- guess and check
- logical reasoning
- choose the correct operation

Math skills

students will use:

- multiply two-digit by one-digit numbers
- add numbers

Restating the problem: Sam took 30 shots but scored 0 points. How many baskets did he make? How many times did he miss?

Important information found in the problem:
- A team earns two points for each basket a player makes.
- A team loses three points for each basket a player misses.
- Sam took 30 shots.
- Sam scored zero points.

Answer Key

Sam made 18 shots and missed 12 shots.
Sam took 30 shots all together (12 + 18 = 30).
He scored 36 points (18 x 2 = 36).
He lost 36 points (12 x 3 = 36).
He earned 0 points all together (36 − 36 = 0).

Bonus Box answer:

9 shots made (18 points) + 0 shots missed
   (−0 points) = 18 points.
8 shots made (16 points) + 1 shot missed
   (−3 points) = 13 points.
7 shots made (14 points) + 2 shots missed
   (−6 points) = 8 points.
6 shots made (12 points) + 3 shots missed
   (−9 points) = 3 points.

Helpful Hints

Share this information when students get stuck to help put them back on the path to correctly solving the problem.

Hint 1 Sam earned zero points. What does that tell us about the number of points he earned and the number of points he lost? *(They are the same.)*

Hint 2 Sam took 30 shots all together. What does that tell us about the number of baskets he made and the number of baskets he missed? *(The sum of the 2 numbers equals 30.)*

Hint 3 Guess the number of baskets Sam made and the number he missed. Remember that the two numbers must total 30. Figure out how many points he earned and lost. Are the numbers the same? If not, adjust your numbers until you find the correct ones.

An All-Star Challenge

Sam loves basketball. When he isn't watching it on television, he's playing it at the gym.

The league that Sam plays for has a different scoring system. A team earns 2 points for each basket a player makes. The team loses 3 points for each basket a player misses. The rules are tough, but Sam likes a challenge.

In one home game, Sam was so eager that he took 30 shots! Unfortunately, he scored 0 points.

When the game was over, Sam couldn't believe that his score was so low. How could that have happened?

Later that night, Sam sat down to figure out how he ended up with such a low score. He just had to figure it out before the next game. His life as an all-star basketball player depended on it!

Now It's Your Turn
Help Sam figure out how many shots he made and how many he missed.

Bonus Box: List 4 ways that Sam could earn more than 0 points if he took 9 shots.

Math Mania

Guessing and checking number combinations to equal a given total

Teacher Page

Problem-solving strategies

students could use:
- choose an operation
- make an organized list
- guess and check

Math skills

students will use:
- add, subtract, multiply, and divide
- solve for missing addends

QUESTIONS ANSWERED

Ravens	0
Hawks	0
Eagles	0

Restating the problem: If each team answered no more than ten questions during each round, how many questions could each team have answered during Rounds 1 and 2 to obtain its total points?

Important information found in the problem:
- Round 1 questions are worth four points each, and Round 2 questions are worth five points each.
- The Ravens have 74 points, the Hawks 71 points, and the Eagles 69 points at the end of Round 2.
- No team answered more than ten questions in either round of play.

Answer Key

Ravens—16 questions (6 questions x 4 points = 24 points; 10 questions x 5 points = 50 points; 24 + 50 = 74)

Hawks—16 questions (9 questions x 4 points = 36 points; 7 questions x 5 points = 35 points; 36 + 35 = 71)

Eagles—15 questions (6 questions x 4 points = 24 points; 9 questions x 5 points = 45 points; 24 + 45 = 69)

Bonus Box answer: Ravens—104 points (5 questions x 6 points = 30 points; 74 + 30 = 104)
Hawks—95 points (4 questions x 6 points = 24 points; 71 + 24 = 95)
Eagles—111 points (7 questions x 6 points = 42 points; 69 + 42 = 111)
The Eagles won.

Helpful Hints

Share this information when students get stuck to help put them back on the path to correctly solving the problem.

Hint 1 Begin with the Ravens. Guess how many questions could be answered in each round of play. Remember that no more than ten questions were answered correctly per round.

Hint 2 Determine how many total points would be awarded in each round. *(Multiply Round 1 questions by 4 points and Round 2 questions by 5 points.)*

Hint 3 Check to see if the total equals 74 points. If not, adjust your guesses and check again.

Hint 4 Repeat the steps for the Hawks and the Eagles.

Math Mania

POW! #39

Well, folks, here we have it! Another exciting game of Math Mania is at hand. Today's game is a heated match between the Ravens, Hawks, and Eagles.

For our audience, let me quickly remind everyone of the rules. Teams receive points every time a question is answered correctly. Questions during Round 1 are worth 4 points each, Round 2 questions are worth 5 points each, and Round 3 questions are worth 6 points each. In addition, each team member is awarded one arcade token for every question answered correctly by his team.

QUESTIONS ANSWERED
Ravens   0
Hawks   0
Eagles   0

At the conclusion of Round 2, the Ravens lead with 74 points. The Hawks are trailing with 71 points, and the Eagles are close behind with 69 points.

Wait! What's happening? It appears that we have a serious problem on our hands. The scoreboard has been erased! Unfortunately, the game has moved so quickly that we can't remember how many questions were answered by each team. However, we do know that no team answered more than 10 questions correctly in either round of play.

With only a few minutes left before Round 3, can the scoreboard manager save the day by getting the scoreboard up and running again?

Now It's Your Turn
Help the manager figure out how many questions each team answered correctly in Rounds 1 and 2.

Bonus Box: In Round 3, the Ravens answered 5 questions correctly, the Hawks 4, and the Eagles 7. What was the final score of each team? Who won the game?

Snack Attack!

Using clues to find the number of cookies the ants collected

Teacher Page

Problem-solving strategies
students could use:
- logical reasoning
- draw a picture
- look for patterns
- guess and check
- work backward

Math skills
students will use:
- use patterns
- add and subtract
- use multistep equations
- divide quantities in half

Restating the problem: The ants visited a picnic site three times to get cookies. On the first trip, they took one-half of the pile of cookies, plus one more. On the second trip, they took one-half of the remaining cookies, plus three more. On their last trip, they grabbed one-half of the pile, plus five more, leaving no more cookies. How many cookies did the ants take in all?

Important information found in the problem:
- The ants made three trips.
- On the first trip, they took one-half of the pile, plus one more.
- On the second trip, they took one-half of the pile, plus three more.
- On the third trip, they took one-half of the pile, plus five more.
- No cookies were left after the last trip.

Answer Key Written explanations may vary. The ants brought 54 cookies home from the picnic.
$54 - (54 \div 2 + 1) = 26$ cookies left after the first trip
$26 - (26 \div 2 + 3) = 10$ cookies left after the second trip
$10 - (10 \div 2 + 5) = 0$ cookies left after the third trip

Bonus Box answer: Trip 1: 84 ants; the ants carried away 28 cookies; 28 x 3 = 84
Trip 2: 48 ants; the ants carried away 16 cookies;
16 x 3 = 48
Trip 3: 30 ants; the ants carried away 10 cookies;
10 x 3 = 30

Helpful Hints
Share this information when students get stuck to help put them back on the path to correctly solving the problem.

Hint 1 The ants took one-half of the pile on their final trip. Then they took five more cookies. No cookies were left. Were there more than five cookies in the pile before the ants took one-half of them? *(Yes, because they took $\frac{1}{2}$ plus 5 more.)*

Hint 2 If there were five cookies left after the ants took one-half of the pile, how many were there when they arrived? *(10)* How do you know? *(If 10 were in the pile and the ants took $\frac{1}{2}$, 5 would be left. Five is $\frac{1}{2}$ of 10.)*

Hint 3 On the second trip the ants took one-half of the pile, plus three more. You know ten cookies were left after they took all the cookies. How many cookies were in the pile before they took the extra three? *(13; 10 + 3 = 13)*

Hint 4 If there were 13 cookies left after the ants took one-half of the pile, how many were there when they arrived? *(26; 13 +13 = 26; 13 is $\frac{1}{2}$ of 26)*

Hint 5 On the first trip the ants found the pile of cookies. They took half, plus one more. After the first visit, there were 26 left. How many cookies were there before they took one extra? *(27; 26 + 1 = 27)* If half of the original pile was 27 cookies, how many were in the original mound? *(54; 27 + 27 = 54; 27 is $\frac{1}{2}$ of 54)*

POW! #40

Snack Attack!

The sun was shining and there wasn't a cloud in the sky. It was a beautiful day for a picnic! Luckily for the ants, the Gowdy family thought so as well!

Not far from the anthill, a red-and-white checkered blanket was nicely spread with all kinds of picnic goodies. The Gowdys were in the nearby meadow flying kites. With the family busy, the ants marched off to gather their feast.

The ants headed straight for the heaping mound of cookies in the middle of the blanket. Before the family could notice, the ants had carried away $\frac{1}{2}$ of the cookies, plus 1 more. They gave the queen all the goodies when they returned. She was very pleased. She told them to go back to the picnic and bring back more cookies.

This time the ants grabbed $\frac{1}{2}$ of the remaining pile, plus 3 more. The queen smiled a very big smile when she saw the cookies. Greedily, she asked her workers to go back and get even more.

The faithful ants did exactly as she asked and returned once more to the picnic spread. This time they grabbed $\frac{1}{2}$ of the pile, plus 5 more. The queen was waiting for them when they arrived. She was about to tell them to head back for more when the littlest ant stepped to the front of the group. Softly she told the queen that there were no cookies left on the blanket.

So the ants all headed down into the anthill to feast on their treats!

Now It's Your Turn
Help the queen figure out how many cookies the ants brought back to the anthill.

Bonus Box: If it takes three ants to carry one cookie, how many ants had to go on the first trip? The second trip? The third trip?

More great math books from *The Mailbox*®

Managing Editor: Irving P. Crump

Editor at Large: Diane Badden

Staff Editors: Denine T. Carter, Kelli L. Gowdy

Writers: Abby Karp (Concept Writer), Bonnie Baumgras, Gina Brooks, Vicki Dabrowka, Rusty Fischer, Ann Hefflin, Geoff Mihalenko, Laura Mihalenko

Copy Editors: Sylvan Allen, Karen Brewer Grossman, Karen L. Huffman, Amy Kirtley-Hill, Debbie Shoffner

Cover Artist: Barry Slate

Art Coordinator: Nick Greenwood

Artists: Pam Crane, Theresa Lewis Goode, Nick Greenwood, Clevell Harris, Ivy L. Koonce, Sheila Krill, Clint Moore, Greg D. Rieves, Rebecca Saunders, Barry Slate, Donna K. Teal

Typesetters: Lynette Dickerson, Mark Rainey

President, The Mailbox Book Company™: Joseph C. Bucci

Director of Book Planning and Development: Chris Poindexter

Book Development Managers: Elizabeth H. Lindsay, Thad McLaurin, Susan Walker

Curriculum Director: Karen P. Shelton

Traffic Manager: Lisa K. Pitts

Librarian: Dorothy C. McKinney

Editorial and Freelance Management: Karen A. Brudnak

Editorial Training: Irving P. Crump

Editorial Assistants: Hope Rodgers, Jan E. Witcher

Manufactured in the United States
10 9 8 7 6 5 4 3 2 1